Rebellious Bodies and Radical Acts

Table of Contents

Introduction
    Alex Bulmer and Debbie Patterson   7

An Urgent Call for the Inclusion of Disabled Artists in Canadian Theatre
    Debbie Patterson   11

Excerpt from *How It Ends*
    Debbie Patterson   17

Deconstructing Ableism
    Yolanda Bonnell   22

Where Liberation Is Expected
    In Conversation with Patty Berne   29

Excerpt from *Stages of Grief: Crip Hearts on Fire*
    Maria R. Palacios   37

Presence as Performance
    Salima Punjani and Karina Iskandarsjah
    Photographs by Mariam Magsi   46

Artist Audience :: Audience Artist
    Alice Sheppard   52

A Practice in Romance
    In Conversation with Vivi Dabee   60

A Meditation on Snakes and Sightlessness
    Vivi Dabee   69

Garden Knows
    JD Derbyshire   72

Excerpt from *Certified*
    JD Derbyshire   80

Access and Intimacy
    In Conversation with Andrew Gurza   84

Excerpt from *Access Me*
    Boys in Chairs Collective   96

Anybody Is an Artist
> In Conversation with Niall McNeil   100

Excerpt from *Beauty and the Beast: My Life*
> Niall McNeil   106

Navigating the Portal: A Deaf Artist's Journey Through the Pandemic
> Chris Dodd   111

Regrowth
> Chris Dodd   117

A Dramaturgy of the Senses
> In Conversation with Audrey-Anne Bouchard   123

Excerpt from *Camille: The Story*
> Audrey-Anne Bouchard   136

Black and Indigenous Disabled Magic, Creativity, and Practice: Defining Our Work on Our Own Terms
> Dr. Syrus Marcus Ware in Conversation with Theodore Walker Robinson and Raven Davis   143

Excerpt from *Antarctica*
> Dr. Syrus Marcus Ware   153

Breaking Barriers: My Journey from Saskatchewan to Shakespeare and Beyond
> Dawn Jani Birley   163

Excerpt and Notes from *Prince Hamlet*
> Why Not Theatre   182

Taking Up Space in an Ableist World
> In Conversation with April Hubbard   188

Dancing Into Connection
> In Conversation with Christopher DeGuzman   199

Conclusion
> Alex Bulmer   208

Perceptual Archaeology (or How to Travel Blind)
> Alex Bulmer   210

About the Editors   249

About the Contributors   250

Introduction
Alex Bulmer and Debbie Patterson

Welcome!

This book is by artists. It is an anthology of essays, scripts, interviews, poetry, and critique by d/Deaf, Disabled, Mad, Chronically Ill, and Neurodivergent artists whose work has advanced the practice and form of theatre and performance across Canada, across Turtle Island, and beyond.

Such diversity of expression reflects our values of accessibility and creative disruption; each artist was invited to reflect on their work or practice through a series of provided prompts, and they contributed through a chosen form that best met their creative and life needs. The resulting publication, like its contributors, is irregular magnificence.

As co-editors, we have gathered some of the most innovative minds working in the realm of disability theatre today, asking each to peel back the curtain on the creative process for Disabled artists engaged in the practice of performance. As performers, our bodies – and our abilities – must be used as the raw material of our craft.

We infuse our work with such embodied perspective and aesthetics – our art may best be described in the words of Sean Li, a Disabled visual artist who calls it 'the last of the truly avant-garde.'

The centrepiece of this book is the complete text of the 2023 production of *Perceptual Archaeology (or How to Travel Blind)*, by Alex Bulmer. It is a richly layered exploration of perception and travel, a journey into unknown geographic and sensorial territory, gathering knowledge through textures and sound, finding presence within the absence of familiar place.

We created this book for our community, to showcase the remarkable work Disabled artists are engaging in, to forward the discourse on this vibrant discipline, and to connect with Disabled and non-Disabled readers.

It is also for those interested in theatre, or seeking to travel through new and unfamiliar territory. Wherever you land, welcome to our space, place, and artistic home.

There is vocabulary used within the book that may need some clarity and context.

Here are a few expansions on terminology that may be unfamiliar to some readers.

Crip Arts/Performance – The word *Crip* comes from the ableist and derogatory English-language word *crippled*. It was used in Western cultures to historically stigmatize and marginalize Deaf and Disabled people.

Crip has been reclaimed by many with lived experience of disability, as a rebellion against the oppression inherent in the word and its negative social and linguistic impact.

'Crip' art and performance refers to work led by Disabled artists centring disability and accessibility as part of the artistic process, practice, and aesthetics of any creation.

Social Model of Disability – The social model of disability (versus the medical model) emerged through the Disability Rights Movement of the 1970s and '80s. It views disability not as an individual's impairment, but as a result of societal barriers and attitudes that prevent Disabled people from participating fully in society. It shifts the focus from what is 'wrong' with the individual to what we need to change to be a more inclusive society.

Disability Justice – Disability Justice is a movement created and launched to the wider world in 2005 by Sins Invalid, a collective of Disabled queer women of colour, including the late Patty Berne (a contributor to this book), Mia Mingus, and the late Stacey Milbern. It builds on the social model and the Disability Rights movement and asserts the need to recognize the intersectionality of Disabled people who belong to marginalized communities, including people of colour, women, transgender people, queer people, Indigenous people, incarcerated people.

Disability Justice seeks inclusion of a person's full and whole self, expecting access and inclusion through a recognition of multiple identities.

Creative Enabler – Inspired by many – including in 2004 by the late British Disabled actor Peter Edwards, with community allies Claire Saddleton and Michael Achtman – a creative enabler is a person who brings a combination of creative, artistic, and access support skills into a performance space. Such artistic interdependence has decades of history within multiple art forms, and other terminologies are used to capture this, such as *artistic connector* or *inter-artist*.

We (Alex and Debbie) both have a long history in theatre and a long adult history with disability. The curation of this book not only showcases and highlights the artists within, but further establishes our community's cultural value and history. Disability has too long been limited within the frame of individual suffering, medicine, and health. Constructed narratives, told by non-Disabled people, have reduced our experience into one of two dreary characterizations: heroes overcoming our broken bodies or victims who can't. The language used to mark the presentation of our work too frequently overexceptionalizes us, erases our cultural past with such slogans as *First ever* or *History starts now*, or undermines our professionalism with assumptions of savant-like magical abilities, achieved without effort, discipline, or rigour. All of us are original, artistry is original, and all great artists make it look easy. Deaf and Disabled artists were not born yesterday, and we are not going away.

Still, the passing of community friends reminds us how valuable and fleeting this earthly time together is. With love, we dedicate this anthology to JD Derbyshire and Patty Berne, both pillars of creativity, and contributors who passed during the production of this book.

Their legacy, like this book, is community. Hundreds of Deaf and Disabled artists not found between these covers could fill a thousand more pages. We may begin to imagine *Rebellious Bodies and Radical Acts, Second Edition*. For now, meet these brilliant artists and enjoy this book!

Accessibility Team: Cindy Boscow, Joanna Hawkins, Dr. Becky Gold, Michael Achtman, Julia Fronduti, Karina Camarena Heredia, Joan McNeil

Many Thanks To: Ravi Jain, Nomy Lamm, and Dr. Jessica Watkin, and to Catherine Frazee for her lifelong contribution to Disability Arts in Canada, which has so deeply impacted our past and future.

An Urgent Call for the Inclusion of Disabled Artists in Canadian Theatre

Debbie Patterson

I've been a working theatre professional since the mid-eighties. About fifteen years into my career, I was diagnosed with multiple sclerosis, which has transformed my abilities and my artistic practice. I'm currently a full-time wheelchair user with an artistic practice that is more focused and vision-driven than ever before in my life.

When I first started experiencing the effects of multiple sclerosis, even though they were very mild, I thought I had to quit working professionally. All my training had been very physical. I believed actors needed to be physically versatile in order to work professionally. I didn't think audiences wanted to see physically disabled bodies onstage. I didn't think directors would be interested in working with actors with physical disabilities. I assumed the ableism in theatre was justified: Just as you wouldn't hire a blind bus driver, why would you hire a Disabled actor?

I decided to transition to directing and writing – aspects of live theatre that I could still do while remaining comfortably seated. But I missed performing. I tried various strategies to work around my disability, to keep acting 'in spite of' my disability, but it all felt awkward and disingenuous.

One day I was in New York and had just been to see Cirque du Soleil. I was still walking with the use of forearm crutches. I arrived at a restaurant where I was meeting some friends. It was kind of cramped, and when I walked through the restaurant, I noticed that the other diners were on high alert. People were shuffling their chairs or moving their bags or coat-tails in order to make sure I had room to get through. It struck me as funny that they would make such a fuss. But I also recognized that the feeling they had watching me walk through the room was the feeling I had had watching acrobats earlier that day. Seeing a person risking a fall, stretching themselves to the limit of their abilities, is compelling no matter where the limit of the abilities lands. That was the day I realized that there was something compelling about the way I move, that the story my body was telling was a story people wanted to hear.

Theatre happens in the body. When we watch theatre, we are watching bodies onstage. The body of an actor tells a story the moment they walk onstage, whether they mean to or not. A person's age, gender, size, colour, rhythm, hairstyle, fashion sense, areas of tension, gait – all these things tell an audience something about who we are. And when we go to the theatre, we are physically present with our bodies in space sharing space with the performers. When a performer speaks, they use their body to create vibrations that travel through the air and enter into our bodies as sound. It is an intimate physical exchange. We breathe together, our hearts sync up, we respond viscerally to each other.

As I learned to embrace (rather than reject, deny, minimize, or try to hide) the transformation of my abilities and the story my body was telling, I discovered the benefits of disability to my artistic practice. I felt I tapped into a deeper authenticity. Disability doesn't let you get away with artifice. You can't pretend to be something you're not. Disability demands a kind of honesty and vulnerability I had never been able to access before. As a woman, I felt freed from judgment about my physical appearance. As an able-bodied performer, I was never able to shake off the feeling that aspects of my body were being judged, held up against some societal ideal of feminine beauty. Once I became Disabled, I no longer felt like I was 'on display,' with no agency in defining what sort of image I wanted to present. There was no longer an ideal that I was supposed to be striving for. I could just be who I was.

In my daily life, I found myself having to take greater risks: doing things physically that I wasn't sure I would be able to do safely. Things like crossing the street, working with power tools, carrying hot things in the kitchen. All these things I did routinely in my daily life prior to

Rebellious Bodies and Radical Acts

Deaf and Disabled Artists Raise the Curtain on Cripping the Stage

Edited by Alex Bulmer and Debbie Patterson

Coach House Books, Toronto

copyright © the contributors, 2026
collection copyright © Coach House Books, 2026

first edition

Published with the generous assistance of the Canada Council for the Arts and the Ontario Arts Council. Coach House Books also acknowledges the support of the Government of Canada through the Canada Book Fund and the Government of Ontario through the Ontario Book Publishing Tax Credit.

LIBRARY AND ARCHIVES CANADA CATALOGUING IN PUBLICATION

Title: Rebellious bodies and radical acts : deaf and disabled artists raise the curtain on cripping the stage / edited by Alex Bulmer and Debbie Patterson.
Names: Bulmer, Alex, editor, author. | Patterson, Debbie, 1966- editor, author | Container of (work) Bulmer, Alex. Perpetual archaeology.
Identifiers: Canadiana (print) 20250315904 | Canadiana (ebook) 20250318504 | ISBN 9781552455135 (softcover) | ISBN 9781770568792 (EPUB) | ISBN 9781770568785 (PDF)
Subjects: LCSH: Actors with disabilities—Canada. | LCSH: Disabilities in the theater—Canada. | LCSH: People with disabilities and the performing arts—Canada. | CSH: People with disabilities, Writings of, Canadian (English)
Classification: LCC PN1590.H36 R43 2026 | DDC 792.087/0971—dc23

Rebellious Bodies and Radical Acts: Deaf and Disabled Artists Raise the Curtain on Cripping the Stage is available as an accessible ebook: ISBN 978 1 77056 879 2 (EPUB), 978 1 77056 878 5 (PDF)

Purchase of the print version of this book entitles you to a free digital copy. To claim your ebook of this title, please email sales@chbooks.com with proof of purchase. (Coach House Books reserves the right to terminate the free digital download offer at any time.)

disability suddenly became risk-filled adventures. This capacity for taking risks fed into my work as an artist, giving me greater freedom to explore in the unknown.

I learned to embrace the disruptions of disability as opportunities for invention rather than barriers to artmaking. If you need to get from one side of the stage to the other and you can walk, then that's the choice you will make. Every. Single. Time. Once you can't walk, every other possible way of getting from one side of the stage to the other suddenly becomes available to you. Now, instead of walking, you might crawl, roll, slither, shoosh on your bum, walk on your hands, ride on something with wheels (e.g., wheelchair, skateboard, scooter), be carried, etc. The disruptions of disability give way to limitless possibility.

Theatre is ultimately a storytelling medium, and narratives have power to change society. Stories shape our beliefs, and beliefs guide our actions. The stories we tell matter. It has been proven that the act of telling one's own story can have positive physiological effects, such as relieving anxiety, improving health outcomes, or reducing pain. Stories have tremendous power.

When Disabled people are excluded from our storytelling mediums, our lived experience is never represented. When every story about disability is created by people without disabilities for people without disabilities, we are misrepresented.

I decided to start a disability theatre company in order to support the development of Disabled theatre artists and the development of stories from the perspective of the lived experience of disability. I felt extremely privileged that I had had the opportunity to get formal training and reach a level of experience prior to becoming Disabled. I wanted to use that privilege in the service of others.

From the outset I was acutely aware that most people would assume a disability theatre company would be providing therapeutic recreational activities for Disabled people. No one would assume that Disabled performers would be exploring complex ideas through a sophisticated aesthetic aimed at giving audiences a powerful experience of self-discovery.

One of the first things we produced at Sick + Twisted Theatre was a cabaret called *Lame Is…* (pun intended). The goal was to redefine disability on our own terms. All of the emerging Disabled performers were paired with mentors who had either a lived or shared experience of disability as well as an established professional practice in theatre. Mentors supported the development of the individual pieces that would be performed in the cabaret as well as mentoring the artists themselves.

Performers were given free rein to create whatever they felt called to do, with three important caveats:
- they were not permitted to create a piece aimed at 'raising awareness' about their particular disability,
- they were not permitted to use the time to complain or perform suffering,
- they were discouraged from being content to simply express themselves and encouraged instead to consider what the audience needs to experience.

These limitations were grounded in the belief that, as Disabled artists, we have a window on an aspect of the human condition that is underexplored in our storytelling media. We also believe that our experience of the human condition is deeply necessary for all people to understand themselves and their bodies in our world. We would mine the depths of our lived experience to excavate precious treasures. We would use our disabilities to help non-Disabled people recognize themselves in a new way.

We knew that people would be coming to our first production with a certain set of assumptions and expectations. We wanted to undermine those assumptions and challenge those expectations.

And we did. Audiences were blown away. My favourite response was 'I'm not sure what I thought I was coming to see, but it certainly wasn't that.' They had never heard Disabled people speak intimately about the experience of disability, about the way we negotiate with vulnerability, about the ways our bodies and brains surprise and delight us. The response told me that we had succeeded in introducing them to parts of themselves they didn't know they were missing.

Disabled artists have been so excluded from our storytelling mediums that the simple act of telling stories from the perspective of a lived experience of disability is a radical act. When we are excluded, stories about us fail miserably.

I was recently at a conference where I was on a panel with another playwright. We were discussing theatrical adaptations of existing works. He was speaking about a memoir he had adapted for the stage that was written by the father of a severely Disabled son. In the process of adapting the play, he interviewed the child's mother, who expressed a desire to outlive her Disabled son. She wanted her son to die before she did. This playwright saw this expression as an act of generosity or selflessness on the part of the mother. This is how he represented disability in his adaptation of this book.

He went on to describe another play he had written about Tracy Latimer's father, who had killed his Disabled daughter at the age of twelve in what he believed to be an act of love and mercy. As a person with a disability, I obviously have strong opinions about leniency toward parents who kill their Disabled children, or romanticizing a parent's death wish for their child. We know that the vast majority of parents who murder their children claim to have acted in the child's best interests. We also know that the judge or jury rarely believe them, unless the child in question is Disabled.

Rather than seeing a parent's death wish for their child as heroic, I see evidence of a sick society that doesn't support the needs of Disabled children and the families who love them. I see a world where parents of Disabled children are isolated by an unnameable aggressive hatred they perceive directed toward their children. I see a world where the thought of abandoning one's child to that unnameable aggressive hatred is inconceivable.

This playwright spoke further about a play he wrote about the Holocaust. Perhaps he was unaware that the first victims of the Nazis' eugenics agenda were Disabled children. The first gas chambers were built in the hospitals where Disabled children were taken for 'treatment.' The Nazis' propaganda campaign against 'useless eaters' targeted Disabled people as a drain on society's resources. Disabled people were dehumanized in order to more easily dispose of them.

It's important to recognize that when we presume to decide whose life is worth living and whose is not, we open the door to all manner of fascism. Ableist attitudes and policies don't just affect Disabled people – they hurt all of us.

As we watch with horror the rise of the far right, we can see once again how assaults on human dignity are being normalized. In this context, the importance of centring Disabled artists, writers, and thinkers takes on a new urgency. Ableism declares that our worth as human beings is based on our ability to produce. It reduces us to wealth-generating units in a capitalist system that seeks to exploit our labour to accumulate resources. Ableism makes us all fearful or ashamed of our basic human messiness. But when we deny our messiness, we deny our humanity. Many of us are driven to ridiculous lengths to overcome or conceal or deny any sign of weakness, aging, or imperfection. All of this prevents us from knowing ourselves deeply, living freely in our messy human bodies.

This is why theatre created by Disabled artists is so vitally important. We need to be telling stories from our point of view. Stories shape our beliefs, and beliefs guide our actions. Our stories have power. Our audiences need to have their internalized ableism challenged in order to free themselves to be who they are. The audiences we are performing for may not be Disabled. Yet. But they do have imperfect bodies. They have vulnerabilities. They all need to know that they are worth more – much more – than their ability to produce. They need to know that they are worthy of care. They need to know that their weaknesses are as important as their strengths in building strong webs of interdependence within their families and communities.

They need Crip wisdom. They need us making art and telling stories. And we must be ready to answer the call.

Excerpt from *How It Ends*
Debbie Patterson

How It Ends is an interactive, immersive, site-specific dance theatre piece that explores end-of-life choices. The script was developed through a series of interviews, and used verbatim and original text. It premiered in April 2019, produced by Sick + Twisted Theatre, presented by Prairie Theatre Exchange.

The Angel appears with a box of shredded toilet paper on her lap. As she speaks, she tosses toilet paper into the air, festooning the audience.

ANGEL: Dignity! Dignity! We all want dignity! Here's some dignity for you. And some dignity for you. And more tattered shreds of dignity for you! Etc.

People talk endlessly about dignity, but when they use that word, we know what they're really saying: 'I don't want anyone wiping my ass.'

'I'd rather die!'

How much time do you spend each day wiping your butt? Have you ever timed yourself? Does anyone know, to the second, how long it takes them to wipe their own ass?

Well then, let's find out. Let's play a game called Wipe Your Butt. Just grab a little shred of dignity and then fold, wrapped or scrunch, as you do. And once you're ready, we'll start the clock. Ready?

On your marks, get set, wipe your butt! (One motorboat, two motorboats, three motorboats, etc.)

If no one will wipe their butt, add this text:

Come on, wipe your butts!

I can't believe you are so reluctant to wipe your butts. Isn't that a valuable part of your day, an activity that you particularly enjoy?

The Angel will try to get someone else to wipe their butt as she times them by counting motorboats. If this doesn't work, the Angel will wipe her own butt, counting out the motorboats as she does.

One motorboat, two motorboats, three motorboats, four motorboats. And then you check. Oh, I have to go again. Five motorboats, six motorboats, seven motorboats, and then you check again. One more and I should be good. Eight motorboats, nine motorboats, ten motorboats, eleven motorboats. And I'm done! Eleven seconds. It only takes eleven seconds to wipe your butt.

But wait. You might do your number two more than once in a day. If you go twice that's 22 seconds, three times that's 33 seconds, four times at 44 seconds, five times – Wait. Nobody does number two more than four times a day. Not on average. So, maximum 44 seconds.

But wait. If you're the kind of person who sits down to pee, you're going to have to wipe then too. How long does it take you wipe the front bum? *(She seeks input from the audience. If she doesn't get it, she just makes it up.)* Maybe … seven seconds? Okay. So, in that case you would have 11 seconds for your first number two, 22 seconds for your second number two, then 29, 36, 43, 50, 57, 64, 71. Just a little over a minute. For the whole day.

But wait, I know what you're thinking! Every now and then it's going to take a little longer, right? When it's that time of the month. How much time does it take then? *(Again, she seeks input from the audience. If she doesn't get it, she just makes it up.)* Should we say maybe 13 seconds? Okay. So, we have 11 seconds for your first number two, 22 seconds for your second number two, and then 35, 48, 61, 74, 87, 100, 113. Under two minutes. Worst-case scenario: you will need two minutes of your day dedicated to butt-wiping.

Sheila enters and begins cleaning up the toilet paper.

I spend two minutes a day doing many things I enjoy. I probably spend two minutes a day laughing. I probably spend two minutes a day reading. I probably spend two minutes a day learning something new. I spend two minutes a day eating something delicious, talking to strangers, cuddling with my sweetheart. There are many things I spend two minutes a day doing that I really enjoy.

But if I can't spend two minutes a day wiping my butt, I'm going to give up on all those other two minuteses. That two minutes of my day is so important that I'm going to call it quits when I can't have that two precious minutes to experience the joy of wiping my own ass.

Man, people must really love wiping their butts. It must be the highlight of their day.

The Angel exits. Throughout the speech, Sheila continues to clean up all the shreds of toilet paper left behind. She arranges eight rolls of toilet paper in a perfect square and stands in the centre.

SHEILA: In any other context, being forced to allow some stranger to remove your clothing and touch your privates would be illegal. If someone doesn't care, if they're perfectly happy to let anyone into their pants, well then, that's fine, that's their business. But that's not me, I don't want to be touched in that way. And if I do not consent, how is that any different from being assaulted? And if I am traumatized by a stranger touching me in an extremely intimate way, that's not me being a prude, that's me being a self-respecting human being. I have boundaries, I don't have to justify them. I wouldn't be called upon to justify my boundaries in any other circumstance. It is unreasonable to subject a person to this kind of assault several times a day, every day, for the rest of their life. For me, being forced into that situation would be nothing short of torture. I value my autonomy and my privacy. I will not be shamed into giving them up. And if I have to sacrifice a couple of weeks of my life in order to maintain my dignity, then it's the price I have to pay. I value my dignity. It is an integral part of who I am.

The Angel enters.

ANGEL: I am what I am what I am what I am. How much do you need to be in control in order to feel like you are who you are? What makes you you?

Bart and Natalie enter. They each take a roll of toilet paper from Sheila's carefully constructed square. They each hand the end of the roll of toilet paper to an audience member and then walk across the circle, draping the toilet paper over Sheila as they cross and handing the other end to another audience member. Through the following, they create a sort of toilet paper pinwheel, with Sheila at the centre. Meanwhile, the Angel goes up to individual audience members and asks them these questions.

ANGEL: What if you had to change your name: would you still be you?

What if you got a face transplant: would you still be you?

What if you had to wear a uniform all the time: would you still be you?

What if you had to move to a foreign country where you didn't know anyone, and you couldn't speak the language: would you still be you?

What if you lost everything you own: would you still be you?

What if you could no longer do your job: would you still be you?

What if you had to spend forty hours a week doing something pointless: would you still be you?

What if you couldn't have sex anymore: would you still be you?

What if you couldn't walk (that's awkward!): would you still be you?

What if you couldn't make things anymore: would you still be you?

What if you couldn't sing or dance anymore: would you still be you?

What if you couldn't remember anything: would you still be you?

What if you were unable to learn new things: would you still be you?

What if you couldn't form complete thoughts anymore: would you still be you?

What if you were shunned by your community: would you still be you?

What if you could no longer express yourself: would you still be you?

What if you couldn't leave the house anymore: would you still be you?

What if you were completely paralyzed: would you still be you?
What if you were in a coma: would you still be you?
WHAT IF YOU WERE IN A COMA: WOULD YOU STILL BE YOU?

The Angel exits.

Deconstructing Ableism
Yolanda Bonnell

Award-winning multi-disciplinary storyteller and creator Yolanda Bonnell hails from Fort William First Nation, and bases their arts practice in land-based creation and Anishinaabe methodologies. Their work has been shortlisted for a Governor General's Literary Award, and earned the Playwrights Guild of Canada Tom Hendry Drama Award. In this chapter, Yolanda shares an original poem and an essay reflecting how their chronic illness reveals the connections between ableism, white supremacy, colonialism, capitalism, and fat phobia.

I'm sorry I didn't reply ...

I was trying to breathe.
I was trying to fill my lungs and fill my lungs
And fill my lungs
And
Move a finger
Or my legs
And the pain –

I'm sorry
I didn't reply, I was working
Still
Working
Still
Because even though we see it – we still feed it.
I'm sorry I didn't reply, I was feeding it.
Not me.

I'm avoiding.
I'm ignoring.
I'm forgetting.
I'm taking more painkillers.
I'll get back to you later-ing.
I'm leaving you on read
Like a terrible friend
No.
No!
I'm trying to survive.
Aiming to thrive.
I'm sorry.

I didn't reply.
There's too much space.
So much space
Out on that highway
And everyone's driving in circles
War on all sides
I'm taking more painkillers.
I'm sorry I didn't reply
I was driving in circles.
Drifting.
Drafting.
Emails – words on a screen. Words I don't recognize.
Words that mean nothing.
No.
No.
They're important.
I'm important.
Feed it.
I'm sorry I didn't reply
I was complaining

*I was tearing up
Gulping down
And down
I was rubbing my eyes out.
Not out.
In.
I was rubbing, scrubbing my eyes.
They're much too dry.
They've been open too long.
Seen too much.
Too much screen time.
Too much
Reflected.
Back.
Smiles and waves.
And
They're receding –
Those waves of creative energy.
They like to wash over me and then leave.
I'm sorry I didn't reply,
I was trying to run out past the break line
I had just enough
Just enough to create this.
And even though I have so much more to say, I'm sorry.
I'm sorry
I didn't reply,
I was doing this instead.*

This is a poem I wrote during a particularly tough breakdown about the inability to function the way I often want to. For me, creation has always been the best way to express the mess on the inside. The mess that has always told me that the way I am inherently isn't good enough. That I have to work harder. Work past the discomfort. Accept the discomfort.

I think many of us grew up with the belief that you can only get to where you want to go with a lot of *hard work* and *rigour*, no matter the cost to your personal being or body. This is a world view that has always excluded – and continues to exclude – Disabled folks from the narrative.

Colonialism.

White supremacy.

Capitalism.

Fatphobia.

All have ableist (and racist) seeds in their cores, and these are the structures we all are forced to live under. Growing up in that mind frame can cause so many harmful perspectives.

For myself, it really had an impact on how I viewed my own body and abilities. I didn't want to be '*crazy*' because I knew the stigma attached to it. I was a fat girl surviving an incredibly traumatic childhood, and as I was entering into adulthood, it all took its toll and severely impacted my mental health.

The structures that held me, and that hold all of us, make us turn on ourselves in brutal ways.

At thirty years old, I attended theatre school and was determined to prove I could do just as much as the twenty-year-olds could do. As much as the thin people could do. And often to my own detriment. There is often a massive lack of empathy toward Disabled folks in general, and I feel like, within the theatre industry, we are often expected to work *through* our disabilities instead of *with* them.

I would push past plantar fasciitis, back pain, eating disorders, and madness just so I could be seen as a 'good actor' – a pliable actor. The actor who doesn't complain, no matter what.

I think being sort of caught up in the whirlwind of the theatre industry right after graduating didn't give me an immediate chance to breathe. I hit the ground running and tried not to think about any discomfort I was feeling because that's how I was trained. To say yes, no matter what. To bend and bend, even if you can't – the show must go on. It was, and is still, colonial and capitalist rhetoric I was indoctrinated into, like many of us are. There has also been *such* a lack of understanding and so much harm working as a racialized person. When I really started to notice these things, I felt like I couldn't unsee them. I was tired of being harmed and watching others being harmed due to the ableist economy, so I started speaking out. Most of it came from my cultural reclamation as an Anishinaabekwe. As my cultural knowledge grew, so did my awareness. Like many of us, I am continuing to still learn and grow and figure out how to build new structures of safe storytelling.

A large part of my artistic process is now based around Disability Justice and compassionate care within theatre. I learned aspects of this from other Indigenous artists, like Dr. Lindsay Lachance and Monique Mojica – who gathered knowledge from Leslie McCue – and I learned a lot from my own harmful, ableist experiences as a performer. I also learned within manidoons collective – the theatre collective I co-artistic lead with Carmen Alvis. I call myself a sovereign storyteller because so much of how I hold space and tell stories is based around Anishinaabe teachings and land-based methodologies. At the core of this practice is deep care for the *humans* – the living beings – who are holding the story. That means ensuring that we're checking in with everyone so we know how to balance the energy in the room, addressing any and all accessibility needs (physical, neurodivergence, moontime, fatness, madness, etc.), having a wellness table stocked with snacks, fidget toys, medicines, etc., utilizing the seven values in the space (humility, truth, courage, love, respect, wisdom, honesty) so we have a framework to follow. We work from where everyone is at, and as a director I will never make a design or aesthetic decision to the detriment of the actors. No one will be made to mine through their trauma for the sake of a performance. They have the freedom to ask for what they need. The team as human beings comes first. Actors, designers, and production teams are not machines. We are actually one large community of people coming together to tell a story. And I feel like the intersection is inside that container of not being recognized as a human.

Outside of the Anishinaabe methodologies, I also have aspects of care woven into the witness/audience interactions. Especially if the work is particularly hard to engage with in terms of triggers, I'll have a healer placed with medicines so there is a space to go to find some healing. I will have the performers introduce themselves and give the trigger warnings before the show begins. Basically, the idea is that all performances are 'relaxed' performances, but even with that, I'm learning that what one group of people feels is relaxed might not be the same for others. So I'm still sorting through how to navigate the many intersections of access needs for the witnesses and working on weaving accessibility measures into the stories I write.

Allowing space for the folks I work with to be their full selves and to just *be* Disabled in the space – to just *be* in general – has also forced me to look at how I'm caring for my own self and body on a daily basis. I think it's so much easier for many of us to show deep care and compassion to the ones around us than to be as generous with ourselves.

I am trying to be patient with myself.
Be compassionate.
Be generous.
Be loving and caring.
With myself.
I want to allow myself to feel the frustration that comes with all of it.
But also allow it to pass through.

I think the pandemic has shifted the conversation about disability in many circles. On one hand, we're seeing far too many people putting others at risk because they refuse to wear masks in public spaces – the individualistic thinking of capitalism overtook any aspect of human kindness and has divided communities. On the other hand, there has also been a lot more discussion around various ways of working – like from home or shorter work hours/days/weeks – which has actually helped the Disabled community.

The one thing that can't be ignored, though, is that the pandemic has caused more folks to become Disabled and has exacerbated everyone's mental health. Mental health/madness can often be left out of disability discussions, and I believe this causes a lot of inner ableism. And it's all easier said than done to deconstruct that inner ableism, but if we're trying to remove these systems that oppress and harm us, then we must also try – at least *try* – to dismantle the internal systems that have been placed there because of them.

We, as Disabled folks – as racialized Disabled folks – as mad and Queer Disabled folks – as fat Disabled folks – and every other intersection that shares the need for Disability Justice – deserve it.

Where Liberation Is Expected

In Conversation with Patty Berne

Internationally acclaimed artist and cultural leader Patty Berne co-founded Sins Invalid, a California-based performance project. Celebrated since 2005 as a primary architect of the Disability Justice movement, Patty led Sins Invalid over two decades of 'Crip Brilliance,' impacting the art and lives of Disabled people world-wide.

In conversation with co-editor Alex Bulmer, Patty shares their lifelong love of live theatre and how they pursued Disability Justice and performance to 'elevate Crips everywhere.' Included is a spoken word excerpt from Sins invalid's 2024 production *Stages of Grief: Crip Hearts on Fire*.

Alex Bulmer: Sins Invalid as a name sure gets your attention.

Patty Berne: Our name is partly due to the strange phenomenon where random people approach a Disabled person and … pray over us.

[They laugh]

AB: Yes, I've been blessed on many street corners.

PB: And we like that people shorten it and refer to us as just 'sins.'

AB: Patty, it's great to talk to you.

PB: I just want to thank you for inviting me to participate in this publication.

AB: Thank you for saying yes. It's a great opportunity to bring community voices together, to have our ideas and creativity collected between the covers of one book.

PB: I like being in good company, with other Disabled artists, particularly mostly marginalized.

AB: Me too. An entire book could be written on you and your work. How do you describe your work and the work of Sins Invalid?

PB: Sins Invalid is a Disability Justice movement and cultural project that celebrates Disabled artists, centring and led by Disabled Black, Indigenous, queer, trans, non-binary, and global majority people.

We understand the work of movement-building to include cultural work. So we understand performance to be a broader and powerful part of this.

AB: I'd like to hear you say more about the intersection of movement-building and cultural work, and why this is so important for you.

PB: I think our survival in part depends on our imaginations, specifically our imagination of different futures. That's why we do social-change work. I'm very grounded in Disability Justice, and that is all about envisioning your future where liberation is expected. You know, some people might call it a pre-formative expectation, but I think we need that. If I didn't think about how things could be, then that would probably be shit, honestly. Because, you know, climate chaos is absolutely on the horizon. Rollbacks on basic health care for people with uteruses. Literal assaults on trans communities, literal assaults on communities of colour, literal assaults on immigrants. And as somebody who comes from a family that immigrated to the United States – I'm Haitian and Japanese, and I'm queer – I exist in a very non-normative body. I've been disabled my whole life, so I've been relying on my imagination to live since I was a child. So, of course, imagination and creativity inform everything for me.

Before we started Sins, I had done some poetry, a little bit of publishing, and worked on films. But Sins is by far the most concentrated body of work I've done, and it's what excites me the most.

AB: Let's talk about the work, and what is exciting for you and Sins at the moment.

PB: We actually do have a show coming up. We're doing a performance on a theme of climate grief. And actually climate rage. So yeah, we're gonna be doing a performance that follows up on our previous performance on climate chaos. Climate chaos is devastating. And we introduced the idea of how devastating it could be for us, because of the systems that have both marginalized us and are not prepared to interact with non-normative bodies, folks who are Disabled or Deaf or Blind. You know, the Federal Emergency Management, or the state, even at the county or city level, they don't know what to do with the Crips. I mean, even hospitals don't know what to do with us, which puts all people with disabilities at huge risk for climate disasters. So, you know, that is reality. We have to envision what could be different for our survival, we need to imagine. And part of that is imagining all of us interacting with the earth differently. All of us are stewarding the land and loving all the other beautiful creatures we're here with, from plants to all the four-legged and winged things. I have a phobia of insects, but I would even say loving insects because of the role they play, and the ecosystems that are staying alive. For most communities in the West, we really have to deepen our relationships in a way that hasn't happened since the Industrial Revolution. Although clearly, communities that are not rooted in Western culture are more likely to have much more significant relationships with the land and everything that she supports.

AB: Are you working to give a voice and a microphone to all you've just mentioned?

PB: In my experience, I think that creatures speak – maybe not English, but they speak. And I wouldn't want to speak for anyone, or anything. I can't say I want to speak on behalf of Disabled people of colour or queer Crips – you know, nobody elected me.

AB: Too bad.

[They laugh]

PB: I'm positioned to speak for myself, and I think that resonates with a lot of people, which is great. If it doesn't, I'd still be saying the same thing. You know the expression 'You're not in the path of truth for lack of people on it.' I believe I've had to learn over years of therapy and surviving trauma that if I don't give what only I can do, it will never be in the history of the planet. What only I can give never has been before. And the same for you. Like, if you don't contribute what only you can contribute, it'll never be. And that would be sad. And I am aware that I'm really fortunate that I have access to some kind of public forum, through my political work and through my cultural work. And I do have something to say. I really do have thoughts and desires and hopes and I want to share them. And I also think about privilege, and what a huge privilege I have. There are so few people in my demographic that have access to health care and education and housing, and I have all of those. On top of that, I have access to some sort of public platform. So I don't want to wait. Privilege, in my opinion, should be used to elevate everyone, and I want to do that. I recognize that even within the U.S. context, I'm multiply marginalized from sources, or in terms of my demographic, but in terms of my individual self, I'm less marginalized than other people in my demographic. Both in the U.S. and absolutely, absolutely globally. Any of us could just as easily have been born into the cobalt mines in Congo, or, you know, I'm Haitian, right, and I could be in Haiti. By whatever is fate, I don't know, the universe has positioned me here. So, of course, I need to use the privileges that I have to elevate Crips everywhere.

AB: Could you tell me more about how you elevate others?

PB: Sometimes directly, by engaging with people and redistributing resources. I think that's very important. Literally elevating other people by helping them with whatever resources I have – be it housing, funds, whatever it is, that's a political commitment. It's a political choice. And sometimes it's offering people a platform through interviews or through sharing their stories. And sometimes it's through just raising awareness, where it wasn't around the circumstances of people's lives. I think it also elevates other people when we engage in a relationship with love. I think love really elevates us. I've worked with survivors of sexual violence for lots of years. The shame we inherit from patriarchy around our bodies when we're assaulted can transform and respond really beautifully to love. I feel like love is a transformational emotion – you know, we are changed by it. And we change others by it. It elevates the vibration, so to speak, of everyone involved.

AB: Patty, you chose to share love and bring others into relationship in many ways, including the arts. Why did you choose the arts?

PB: You know, it reaches people. I think when we can intake something that's not didactic, that's more about beauty, that we're asked to experience in both sides of our brain, it's like it hits our cerebral cortex, our reptile brain. And we respond from there, which is a little torturous, like how it's a little torturous to watch horror movies, because we're responding to it as though it's real, even though we know it's not. The front of our brains take a second to analyze it, but our reptile brain is like, 'Oh shit, there's a three-headed monster.' I'm one of those who likes to watch that. I want our audiences to feel what we're experiencing as Crips, and also experience a new vision for what we could be doing as all people. So yeah, I think it was intentional to use creative work. Also, sometimes, that's the only way we can express ourselves. When I've been in so much pain that I'm near the end of my rope... When I was younger, I really, really, really struggled, and it was incredibly important for me to write and just pour out. I could do it in writing, I certainly couldn't do it verbally. You know, sometimes beauty is so profound we don't have words for it, but we can communicate it non-verbally onstage.

AB: You reach people onstage, but also with your online content. Is there ever conflict between the process, between an urgency to create digital content and a slower, maybe deeper, process to make original theatre?

PB: I do think new media can bridge the deep and the urgent, because you can create art and then put it on social media. And it can then, very quickly, get seen by so many more people than we have in a theatre. So I don't think it's a necessary conflict; I think someone does need to know how to use those tools, because it *is* a tool. It's not unto itself. I think people have had this tension before. Do you remember Warren Beatty?

AB: I remember Warren Beatty!

PB: Yeah. So he said, 'Why do it if it's not on camera?' I'm sure other people have said that before. I just remember him saying it. And, I think, as the technology develops, so does its ability to reach people. Like, before it would be from the pulpit you could reach, you know, a couple hundred people, but now we're reaching a couple thousand, and within moments. So I think whatever technology is available at the day was probably created in order to reach people more and more. Who knows, maybe we'll each have control of a satellite before the earth collapses.

But I will say that our shows are made to be seen live. As a director, I have not made the move to produce a show for live streaming. We're going to edit together a show from the raw footage. We're going to edit together essentially a small film, like we always do, that can be seen online. But the live show is meant to be felt viscerally in the space. Performers are giving energetically, like a ton, a ton. And sometimes you can tell that when you're watching it, but it's harder to feel the effects. It depends, I think, on the performer and on the audience member. But really, live shows are made to be live shows.

AB: I can hear your love of live performance.

PB: Yeah. I grew up in San Francisco, and as soon as I was living on my own, I was sixteen, I was going to shows all the time, at some of the venues we perform at now.

And it was awesome. Going in the evening, and being with other audience members, and then sitting – usually the Crip seating is right in the front. I'm a wheelchair user, so I would sit right in the front. And I was quite shy as a young person. So I would be simultaneously enthralled by being in the front and terrified that I would be seen somehow. That the lights would fall on me, and people would see me or that the performer would in some way respond to me. And that was scary for me, and I think for probably a lot of Crips who have not yet worked through shame. I was just really attracted to it, though – things I had never seen on TV would happen.

AB: What do you mean?

PB: Even just movement. I love dance, and so watching movement. I would watch flamenco a lot. And, man, there's nothing like live flamenco, and the way they riff, people are just jamming. And then also live music similarly – I love jazz. And went to jazz shows when I was sixteen. I think I am trying to recreate some of that now. I mean, what I experienced was sacredness. It's like the same feeling as – not to be weird – but like going to church. Just awestruck at this other non-verbal experience of beauty. I'm really proud that Sins and the performers are able to create that. People are able to create this sacred space.

And sometimes it's devastating. If a performer is talking about their experience of a climate disaster and being left in their home with water rising, and with, you know, FEMA or whoever, whatever federal agency, saying, 'You have to leave your wheelchair or we can't take you,' that's heartbreaking. And this sacred space invites fullness. It's just gorgeous to see a performer fully embodying their beauty, their sexuality, their desire, their self-ownership of their body, and loving themselves. Damn, it's so paradigm-shifting, it's just so hot.

AB: This might be your mic-drop moment.

[They laugh]

AB: Is there anything else you'd like to say?

PB: I think we have a responsibility to move hearts and minds, toward justice, toward love. As creators, as artists, we're changing people. Why not change people for the better?

Excerpt from *Stages of Grief: Crip Hearts on Fire*
Maria R. Palacios, Sins Invalid poet in residence

When a Disabled Person Dies

When Covid hit,
stories of Disabled people being abandoned
pierced my soul
– Disabled people around the world being left to die …
Disabled people who were left behind and starved to death
as non-Disabled family members fell ill, and caregivers and attendants
    had to be quarantined.

Disabled people are always the first to be abandoned.
Lives that could have and should have been saved are discarded and
    thrown away.

Lives like the life of Michael Hickson
who, during Covid, was denied the right to live and was intentionally
    starved
by the medical professionals who saw his life as being empty
of meaning,

they starved him to death
because, as a quadriplegic, they said,
he had no quality of life although he had a wife and a fairly average life
    despite being a quad … (although I've never really known any
    Disabled person to live just an 'average life' … living from one
    minute to the next can be extremely intense when you depend upon
    others to keep existing in your body).

Like him,
there have been many others ...
other Disabled people who died although
they could have been saved,
people whose lives
go unnamed by the non-Disabled because it becomes easier that way
to feel no guilt for what they do to us.

They justify their actions and hold on to their refusal to recognize our
    Disabled lives as lives worth living ... as lives worth saving.

I remember
feeling horrified and terrified
at the realization of how disposable our Disabled lives seem to the world.

We live in danger ... in terrible danger ... and we live in a constant state
    of grief ...
Grief ...
we don't always know where to place or how to make space to heal
    because every single time a Disabled person dies

a part of us dies with them ... a little bit of ourselves
... our own history as Crips gets taken,
the awareness of our own mortality is awakened,
our own relationship with death,
our own relationship with life,
our commitment to love, and everything we love
flashes before our eyes ...

every time a Disabled person dies ...

we mourn, we grieve, we regret
how easily we forget to be more present for each other

while we're still alive
instead of celebrating life
at each other's funerals.

Our funerals are often stained
by ableism.
There will always be those
who celebrate our death
because they think we lived
a life full of dread
having to exist in our Disabled bodies.

Our funerals are often invaded by inspiration porn
from the family members and people who never got to know
who we became as Crips,
saw us as perpetual kids,
infantilized our dreams,
or made us seem like angelic heroes for not hating our lives.

The non-Disabled almost always celebrate our death because it is seen as
    the only way of setting us free
from the misery they imagine our lives were. They think our entire lives
    had only been lived
wishing for non-Disabledness or some form of relief.

Society really does believe
that death, for Disabled people,
is better than living a Disabled life … of any kind …
because Disabled people are always
just better off dead than having to bother the world
with our needs and our pain
and our demands for equality … I mean,
what a burden we must be on them

for wanting to claim the right
to own our bodies,
the right
to own our lives!

When a Disabled person dies … my patience with the non-Disabled world dies a little more … It makes me want to yell out:

NO MORE!!
NO MORE!

No more denying us access to own our bodies.
No more condemning our minds
or diminishing our truths.
No more seeing our struggles as a token you use
to redeem yourselves and make you believe you've done enough
while we continue to suffer, and cry ENOUGH!
No more!

No more of us dying of curable or treatable conditions.
No more being denied care we need and deserve.
No more Disabled lives thrown away, abandoned in institutions, forced to live in poverty and blaming us for it.

No more denying us access to things essential to our survival.

No more having to explain ourselves in normative terms to justify our existence.
No more having to wait for human rights given to us like fucking crumbs while you feast on your privilege.
No more ableist fuckery!
No more medical-model-rooted approach to our survival.

Who the fuck gives YOU the right to decide the value of a life??

We don't have to die like this.
We deserve a chance to live.
We want to live.
We deserve to survive.

Other Disabled people need to know what we've learned.
There are Crips out there so isolated
that they truly believe ableism is all there is
and all that they deserve …

The Crips who survive are the ones who have access
to community, access to someone who gives a fuck …
access to a little bit of luck and connections in the right places
in a world of non-Disabled spaces
and all the ableist crap we have to swallow just to stay alive.

We survive by having to prove our worth
through every word we say and everything we do.

Sometimes we survive by getting used to shit and tuning out oppression,
by justifying it
or finding reasons to believe
what the non-Disabled believe
that way we don't feel so abandoned even though we are.
We survive by having to think outside
the usual box
and having to detox from the trauma of ableism.

Every time a Disabled person dies,
another piece of myself dies with them … I just know I'm not the same.

I know Covid changed us all …
2020 was the year
that broke many of us …
it was the year that broke me and my faith in humanity.
It was the year that left me afraid and devastated … less able to fight.
I had become more exhausted, less able to get back up after each fall –
 unable to give myself whole
when pieces of myself get scattered across the life stories
of other Crips … their deaths
rip me apart, force me to pull myself together with pieces missing from
 my heart.
I manage to create
new versions of myself
through the voice of my art.

That's how I remain whole, mend myself back to usable condition so I
 can embrace the scars, and just try
to keep
on
living.

Crip Resurrection

Crips come back to life after we die,
much to the horror of the non-Disabled.
There's always a new generation
of Crip.

We come back to life
through the next Disabled person, and the next
and the next …
the next car accident,
the next shallow dive,
the next gunshot wound,
the next senseless war.
The next undetected birth defect …
one you will label a wrongful birth …
an error,
a mistake,
but make no mistake:
Crips come back to life
and do so a little savvier each time,
armed with the history of Crip ancestors who paved the road once upon
    an ableist world afraid of Disabled people.

Crips come back to life
because we leave our history
written in blood and drool.
We leave you lessons you'll never learn in school –
the wisdom of our survival passed on to other Crips
like the ancient knowledge of elephants and trees
– wisdom that must be passed on to others
so that we can exist

in future dreams
and future generations of Disabled people.

We leave our history
stitched to the pages of Disabled lives
who would have nothing, otherwise, connecting them to Crip truths.

We *are* Crip truths ...
Crip truths
that get erased or go untold.
We are raw survival,
Crip bodies
and Disabled body-minds
forced into the invisibility
of non-Disabled fear ...
and we are here
surviving against all odds.
We are here
whether you like it or not.
We are crip, brown, and queer,
Crip BIPOC revolutionaries
reclaiming the power
you thought we did not have,
and resurrecting Crip truths you thought
would die with us.

But Crips always come back to life.
We reincarnate ourselves
in the next Disabled life ...
and the next and the next.
We are a never-ending loop of Crip survival.

We tangle our crippleness
around your own lives
and get rooted into the reality of you
as you evolve into Crip
and the very things you feared most …
but fear us not, my loves,
fear us not, for look at us,
we are evidence of evolutionary love,
life-saving love, Crip love,
love capable of healing the wounds of ableism, putting back together
the torn pages of our history
as we rewrite ourselves
into the DNA of *your* own truths.

Crips come back to life.
We are you.
We are one.
Come with me.
(Come) I'll show you the path
leading to your own
Crip resurrection.

Presence as Performance

Salima Punjani and Karina Iskandarsjah
Photographs by Mariam Magsi

Internationally acclaimed, Montreal-based social artist and storyteller Salima Punjani uses multimedia to explore intersections between science and art. Her work has travelled across Canada, to Ethiopia and Japan, and she holds a distinct practice ensuring people actively participate as both subjects and viewers. Below is Salima's summary of her durational work *The Space in Between*, followed by a conversation she had with curator and project supporter Karina Iskandarsjah.

In July 2023, artist Salima Punjani transformed Trinity Square Video in Toronto into something unexpected: a gallery reimagined as a welcoming gathering space. Her relational multimedia art project, *The Space in Between*, invited about thirty artists from Toronto's Mad/Deaf/Disability Arts community to help shape this vision through ten intimate conversations shared over meals.

The transformation began with intention. Before any gathering took place, Punjani and her team developed an access menu – a comprehensive outline of possible accommodations that welcomed input and requests from invited artists. The responses revealed the beautiful complexity of access needs such as specific fidgets and stim materials, visual cues, migraine-friendly lighting, Covid safety, sober-friendly environments, air purifiers, and soft seating arrangements.

Punjani carefully considered each request, weaving these diverse needs into the creation of a cozy living room within Trinity Square Video. Here, she curated and hosted the invited artists for meals and meaningful exchanges, with contact microphones quietly capturing the essence of these encounters. Through vibrotactile technology – which transforms sound into physical vibrations – these recordings became the foundation for a multi-sensory listening experience.

The project reached its culmination in a public exhibition where visitors could inhabit the carefully crafted living space, immersed in the layered sounds of the artist gatherings. What emerged was more than documentation – it was presence as performance, community as art form. This is a conversation between Salima Punjani and curator Karina Iskandarsjah, who supported the project throughout the process.

Karina Iskandarsjah: I thought we could start with talking about the title itself, *The Space in Between*, and how that was a catalyst for a lot of really fun exploration to be had with this concept of in between the lines and between the art. Do you have any initial thoughts on the theme of that title and the main subject matter you wanted to explore and focus on?

Salima Punjani: The idea of *The Space in Between* came from a sense that a lot of the memorable moments of connecting with other Disabled artists happened in between the actual reasons why we were there. I find there's a certain kind of magic to these little in-between moments that are so mundane. These moments were possible because public access costs had been considered. I just wanted to hold space for those in-between times. There wasn't a larger purpose as such than to just be together. We originally programmed this work in between Trinity Square Video's planned exhibitions, as a way of using a gallery in a different way than to necessarily show art – to use it as a way to create social connectedness. It ended up being part of the main programming.

KI: Can you elaborate on your choices in terms of your focus on capturing the in-between moment and the technical routes you chose for that?

SP: In a way, the relationship was the performance. The everyday things were the performance. It almost feels like that kind of presence is the most difficult kind of performance to do. Where it's like, you're there, you're hosting, you're with. I decided to capture these relational moments through contact microphones, which don't necessarily make a beautiful sound but rather capture traces of togetherness like the vibrations of laughter, thumps from knocking the table, and clinks from glasses. I think there's a way to use technology to be more subtle and to actually highlight these little things. The fact that we could all be at the table together, whether online or in person, that's pretty spectacular. It takes a lot to be together as people with different access needs, desires, and frictions, so I wanted to celebrate just that.

KI: There's something about these fundamental and very relatable sounds. There's a lot of gravity to the simplicity of a thump or like the glass is clinking because of the context of the people and the space.

SP: It's not really about technology. It's about the people and their relationships to each other. I think it's pretty amazing that we were able to present this type of durational performance as main programming. Where the participants and viewers actively contributed to the design and experience of the space with their presence. I think there's a lot of value to messing up these arbitrary separations between the artist and the audience.

KI: I think it's really important to mess with those expectations too, like: What is art? Who does it serve? What is its function? Turning a gallery into a living space, you know, conceptually as art, playing with those expectations, was really fun. Everybody really wanted to hang out in the space because it was a living space and not just somewhere you stand for a few moments.

SP: And what kind of spaces get created when we listen to each other and create the space for us to show up as we are as artists, as d/Deaf, Disabled, neurodivergent, immunosuppressed folks? Don't get me wrong, there was friction too. Having folks who have different ways of working and being together – it's not always seamless. But how do you mitigate that and still try to create an environment where there's grace for not being perfect? I definitely felt a lot of pressure to show up for people in the space.

KI: Totally. I think *grace* is totally the right word here, because we did run into a few, I guess, instances of access friction, not just among the guests but also among project team members. There's a lot of discussion right now about masquerading care and not actually doing the care work. And I'm so proud of us, for discussing care and trying to integrate it into the project strategies – even though it wasn't perfect, it really wasn't. I have many regrets about maybe doing so many gatherings in such a short time. You know, 20/20 hindsight … something like that.

SP: Yeah, for sure. I think about some of the things I regret and I think I was just so excited to have the financial capacity to hold space for people that I forgot about what I needed for me as the host/performer. We shifted strategy to adjust and hired extra help, like an access doula for the public events, and that was really helpful. It's very humbling to remember that I'm also a sick person and to admit how much more help I needed than I thought I did. It was interesting to see how there was all this structuring of care for everyone and then realizing just how much is always needed for us too.

KI: On that note, though, do you want to talk about some of the things you would do differently in terms of, you know, being a sick person? Would you let other people host in the future instead of you being the only host?

SP: Absolutely. Actually, something that I would dream of doing is creating the space and then having a bucket of access and hospitality funding that people could just use to self-organize their own gatherings and take turns hosting. People have the power and the agency to create what they want to see. Invite who they want to invite. Where it's *our* performance instead of *my* performance.

KI: What are you leaving the project with?

SP: I leave the project with a better understanding of what it means to create generous, welcoming environments and spaces and the joy and pleasure that comes when it is possible to create the right conditions for connection.

Photo 1: The opening event of the public exhibition, where attendees are gathered in the same intimate living room space that had hosted the original artist conversations. The circle of people sitting on cushions, beanbags, and rugs around a low table demonstrates how the public was invited to inhabit and experience the same communal setting where the recorded conversations took place. The opening attendees are physically occupying the space while being immersed in the sounds of the previous gatherings through the vibrotactile technology, making them both audience and participants in the ongoing artwork.

Photo 2: An industrial gallery with exposed brick walls and dramatic skylights has been converted into a welcoming living room. Visitors can be seen exploring the space, which features comfortable seating arrangements, including a bed with colourful textiles, floor cushions, and a dining table. The contrast between the formal gallery architecture and the intimate domestic furniture captures the project's goal to reimagine institutional spaces.

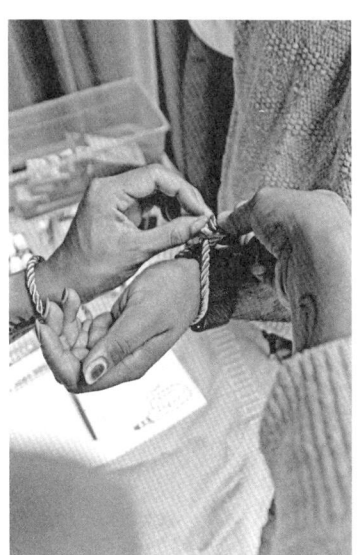

Photo 3: Someone's hands are shown tying a braided silky purple cord around another person's wrist. People were given the option to use wrist ties of different textures and colours to represent their social energy. Blue hard ribbons symbolized a colder, less social energy. The purple cord represented neutral energy and a bright fluffy orange wristband symbolized very social hyper-energy. This is an example of the sensory and tactile experiences within the project, showing how access needs and desires were integrated into the relational experience.

Presence as Performance | 51

Artist Audience :: Audience Artist
Alice Sheppard

Award-winning artist and artistic leader Alice Sheppard has an acclaimed international practice spanning two decades within Disability Arts. As dancer and choreographer, Alice founded and continues to be artistic lead of Kinetic Light, working at the intersections of disability, dance, design, identity, and technology. Below, Alice explores the experience of the gaze of both non-Disabled and Disabled audiences, reflecting her perceptions through poetry.

Grounding

1.

        Centred
        Disability
        Centred

        Access
        Trust
        Access

2.

why
oh
why
do we rely
on the non-disabled

eye?
I
Root
Ground
Find
My
Self
My
I

spy
with my crip eye

3.

Once, I was you.
Neck cricked up.
Senses honing in.
A spasm ripping through
Then braced.
I was out there
Disabled. Needing
Someone to show me
A me beyond myself.

Night after night
Bitter disappointment sliced
Cut after cut.
I was not enough.
Lights up.
Frantic applause.
Silent slivers of flesh.

Give me
Crip art
Gimp performance
Freak show
Disabled worlds

Onstage, I feel your longing –
All hunger, half shame, part hope.
Hi, you.
Out there.
Waiting.
I inhale you.
Then, sync our breaths.

I promise you this,
disabled one.
You are enough
for me.

4.

Access a moving
toward justice and equity.
Move, reach, stretch.
Access this, my friend.
The love of our community
extends beyond doors
through floors
connecting me to you.
Moving with access.

Showtime

5.

Inhale
Fire
Desire
Exhale
Heat.

Heat
A scorching rage for
Accountability
To
Disability.

Inhale
Grace
Space
Exhale
Truth.

Truth
The blazing realization
That
A body does not lie.

But
what if
my bruises, sweat, calluses, and dislocations
my tears, hurt, and joy –
What if my heart, my whispers,
my love,

cannot hold back the
sprain of misconnection.

6.

I trusted you.
I unwrapped my layers
Offered myself.
I committed.

I can't.
I won't.
Don't talk back
with me.

What happened?
Just wondering
Are you actually disabled?
Just curious
What do you eat?
What's wrong?
So inspiring.
How did you?

Screw empathy.
Fuck your compassion.

I trusted you.
I gave you my body.
I arched my spine.
Invited you in.

7.

How did you find me?
How many before me?
How do you leave your loves?
Why did you choose me?
Are you my kin?
Who do you know?
Do you know me?
How do you know me?
Why are you here?
Again

I don't know you
I don't care that you paid
I don't choose you
I don't want you
I don't need you
I do not consent to this.

8.

I love you.
Shimmying in your seat.
Slurping your tea.
Rustling your food wrapper
Jumping up, walking around.
                I love you.
                Beep of your chair horn.
                Snick of your cane.
                Click of your releasing knee.
                              I love you.
                              Meds

                                    Mask
                              Defenders
                                    Cush

                                    Pads
                                   Brace
                               Magnifier
                                   Wipes
                               I love you.

            Clunk of your buckle
          Whirr, hiss of your vent
            Padding of your dog
                 I love you.

Checking, yes, endlessly checking your phone.
Touching your neighbour.
Flopping on your cushion
Fuck yessing aloud.
I love you.

Re Turning and Turning

9.

Sweating
under the sheets
I can't release
the memories sweet.

Replaying
with each swift breath
each little death
the contours of our night.

I came
home alone.

                       Access
                        Trust
                       Access

                       Centred
                     Disability
                     Centred

A Practice in Romance

In Conversation with Vivi Dabee

Scholar and artist Vivi Dabee is the central figure in the 2020 CBC television documentary *Vivi's Vision*. Passionate about inclusion, access, and literacy, she is co-host of the podcast *The Lens: Living Diverse* and is the audio-description consultant for VIEW, Winnipeg's audio description team. In conversation with Alex Bulmer, and through an original creative 'meditation,' Vivi reflects on her experience of sighted assumptions and finds insight from a creature that sheds its skin.

Alex Bulmer: I know you professionally as a scholar and a writer and an actor and a theatre maker, and as a Blind artist, but I'd love to hear in your words how you would define yourself and describe your practice.

Vivi Dabee: I prefer to describe myself as an artist, because I think that term is very fluid and encompasses all the things I do that you just described. So I think that term allows for a lot of flexibility and inclusivity, and depending on who I'm talking to and what I'm working on, I think that's the term that fits me best. I also think it's kind of a romantic term. People think of different things when they think of artists, and so I kind of like that connection to creativity and romance as well.

AB: I have to pick up on your words *romance* and *romantic*. Because when I read your work, I get a really strong sense of writing from the Romantic Period.

VD: That's great to hear. I'm really drawn to literature within that period, the early nineteenth century, late eighteenth century – I would have to look up the dates to be absolutely correct. But it's an area of literature that I studied. So it's definitely where I am drawn and where I like to spend my time thinking and writing and creating.

AB: Why is that?

VD: I think it is the fact that at the time, in my perspective, those authors were so vividly descriptive and so passionate, so connected to their emotions and not afraid of expressing emotions, so connected to their sensitivity and allowing that to come through their work. I claim that identity, and I am proud to say that I'm a very sensitive person. I feel a connection with those authors, and that they grant permission to have all of these feelings, express all of these feelings, and navigate them and negotiate them and just live in them, and they're granting access and permission, and I really like that. I think there's a liberty and a freedom in dwelling – not necessarily wallowing – but dwelling in these emotions and where they take you.

AB: You used the word *permission*. Is being sensitive not always permitted?

VD: Yes, I can remember growing up and being told by certain members of my family, 'You're too sensitive. You don't know how to take criticism. You take everything too personally. You know, your way of being in the world is not the greatest way to be in the world.' Defining what way to be, like what is acceptable – who gets to define what is acceptable? I dwell in the emotional space, and I'm okay with that. I think there's a lot of ableist philosophy that wants you to not be in that space and just be productive and produce and do what you're called to do and not channel those emotions.

I have also received, you know, comments to the contrary, that people appreciate how supportive and emotionally available I am and can be, and have been to them when we're working on things that are highly emotional.

I feel really more at home in the creative, artistic space, and the theatre space. I can be messy and be strange and be weird and all of the things that dominant ableist society would say are wrong with me or wrong with people, and just be loved and accepted, and, you know, welcomed into this wonderful community that I have returned to after a long journey away from it.

AB: There's a story there. What took you away?

VD: You know, Alex, when I first entered the world of artistry and theatre, I was not welcome, not made to feel welcome.

I was in the midst of my undergraduate degree and was studying theatre as my unofficial minor. I had taken theatre classes in my first and second year with the same professor and had registered for a movement class with him. I thought this would be a great idea both from a theatre perspective and a blindness perspective, because one of the skills you learn when you are adjusting to life as a Blind person is orientation and mobility. It is how to navigate the world without relying on your eyes to guide you. I thought that taking a movement class would enhance my bodily and spatial awareness and make me really think about how I was moving and how I wanted to move onstage and through the world.

I did not have the word for it then, but this professor's response to me was extremely ableist. He forced me to withdraw from the class because he thought I would injure myself. I was not a strong self-advocate yet. I felt that the world of theatre did not welcome or want someone like me.

AB: I'm so sorry you were treated that way.

VD: I don't think my experience is unique. I don't know many Blind actors, and I think that is a direct result of being excluded from theatre because of antiquated ableist attitudes. I feel that often when people encounter someone who is blind, they focus on all the things they believe the Blind person cannot do or cannot imagine doing without sight. If a person is uninterested in – or does not want to take the time to learn about – other methods to enable the success of the Blind person, then the Blind person suffers the consequences, and an ableist mentality is perpetuated.

AB: How did you get back to the theatre?

VD: After many years of pursuing other things, literature being one of them, I came back, and I'd say it was in 2019, through playwriting and my Winnipeg Fringe show. I had left the academic space, which is where I was focusing all of my energy, and I was following that career path because I thought, if I couldn't do theatre, I'd do literature.

One of the pieces I had read when I was studying, when I was doing my master's, had just resonated with me so much. And I knew when I had first read it that it needed to be brought to life in some other way. I didn't have the time while I was in school to do that, but then when I left, I started to write this play based on a novella I loved so much.

AB: What is it? Who wrote it?

VD: It's a novella called *Passing* by Nella Larsen, and she is no longer with us.

AB: What about it spoke so strongly to you? You clearly connected with it.

VD: She was a mixed-race author, and I had studied the novella in a class called Literature and Psychoanalysis of Race. So it was kind of exploring race through the lens of Freud and his theories, and I like to look at things through that kind of lens, like a psychoanalytic lens, when I'm reading and writing. And the story is about two mixed-race friends, Claire and Irene, in Chicago during the Harlem Renaissance, and they are childhood friends, and they are separated when they are still young. And one of them, Irene, chooses to embrace her Black identity, and the other one, Claire, because of her life circumstances, chooses to embrace her white identity and pass – hence the title of the book.

She ends up marrying a white man who does not know that she is mixed race because she's just embraced her white identity. However, she has a sense of longing for the side of herself she has not embraced and not, you know, identified with, since she left her childhood friend in Chicago. Eventually, Claire wants to reconnect with Irene, which poses a complication for Irene, because she has identified as Black and now, like, what do you do when someone who you've defined yourself in opposition to now wants to re-enter your life , and re-enter your life in such an intense way. And for me, there are strong connections.

I am also a person of mixed race. I'm not mixed with Black and white, but I have Afro-Caribbean and Indo-Caribbean ancestry. On the surface, that probably doesn't seem like a big thing, but within Caribbean culture, that is a big thing. So, I won't get too much into it, but there's the similar kind of hierarchy where, if you're considered darker skinned or from African descent, in a way you're perceived as less than. So – and also just another layer of passing – before I became blind I was a person with usable sight, and I, at times during my life, pretended to see more than I could. So I saw another element of passing there, which is not indicated in the book, but which I identified with. These things you portray to the world, and then you have to grapple with the reality of your true lived circumstance.

AB: That is exhausting, to keep up such a dual reality.

VD: Absolutely. That is very much in the book, and it really resonated for me.

AB: Okay, so you turn the story into a play …

VD: Yes, and put my name into the Fringe, and I was chosen, and I proceeded to produce my play. However, because of my past experience of being unwelcomed, I really thought, 'Well, I can do theatre, but I can only be backstage, like nobody's gonna want to see me as a Blind actor.' I was presented with the thought that the career path for a Blind person was very limited, and I internalized that. So I thought, 'Okay, at least backstage I can still be connected to the world I love.' But the real gift was when Deb Patterson at Sick + Twisted approached me to be your understudy, Alex, for *Antigone*, playing the role of Tiresias. She approached me and asked, 'Can you sing? Would you be open to being Alex's understudy?' And, of course, I said yes, because nobody calls the understudy. And then you weren't able to come to Winnipeg. So I would say that my return to theatre, where my real passion lives, as an actor, was through the opportunity to play Tiresias when you weren't able to do it.

AB: One of my greatest gifts to others is not showing up. *(They laugh.)* You were very understanding.

VD: We are both guide-dog users.

AB: Yes. The times I've unfortunately not been able to come to Winnipeg have been because of my need for a guide dog. Getting a guide dog is a really hard process. You need to be ready to go with hardly any warning. You get the phone call and you have to drop everything and travel many miles away to a school.

VD: And it's so important that it works out, because the waiting time can be years. It's a major commitment.

AB: Especially within the first year or so, while you are both bonding and team building. Okay, we both have dogs and we're both actors. Tell me about you, the actor, and the techniques you practise as a Blind actor. Especially how you're developing techniques to work with new material.

VD: I'll talk about our recent show, *Neither Here Nor There*, very much a collaboration with Sick + Twisted. I first have to say that I have not worked with, you know, another writer, never mind six or seven or however many of us ended up contributing pieces to that production. And I'm learning as I go, because my return to theatre is, in my mind, relatively recent. So I'm learning that I can ask for things I never thought I could ask for, like a creative enabler. We had one. So that would be our term for someone offering sighted guiding plus all additional sighted support when we're doing the show.

I know when we were doing round one of work and rehearsal, we had one creative enabler who was supporting you and me. Well, I think he was meant to support you, me, and the third Blind actor on the show. And I thought, 'Hmm, I think something here needs to change, because there are three of us who may be needing support at the same time or at different times.' So after speaking to you, Alex, because you have more experience, I felt comfortable and confident to speak to our director, Deb, and say, 'Could it be possible for us to have a second person as a creative enabler, just to support all of the needs of the actors and so that we're not having competing needs, and that one person isn't being pulled in many directions?' And Deb was very receptive and open to that. So I'm learning I can voice my concerns and say what I need, and it's okay to do so even if I'm the only one who needs it. It's all right to raise your voice and speak your needs in terms of the practical process of being a Blind actor.

AB: We used a technique called line feeding.

VD: Yes. I have been introduced to the process of line feeding. So, through the power of technology and human assistance, through much of the rehearsal process, our creative enablers spoke into a device and fed us our lines.

AB: Yes, and there's a little earbud in our ear. You took to it so quickly.

VD: Because I am a strong auditory learner, I found that process really helpful. That's the method I used when I was learning my lines at home. I would have them recorded and then just listen over and over again until they became entrenched in me. I find that process is very helpful to me as a Blind actor. It's also very liberating, because there's no anxiety about, like, 'How am I going to read this? How am I going to learn this?'

AB: What kind of details did you and your line feeder talk about to make it work for you? Did you discuss speed of delivery or breathing?

VD: I think both and – and you're right, it does require some listening between both to make that work. It's kind of an intimate relationship. So we had maybe a few discussions about it, not many, because our creative enabler is a great listener. He's also an actor. And I think he said to me at one point during rehearsal, he could tell when I was going to call for line, because he was paying attention and he was looking at me, and he was tuned into me.

He told me he could see me searching, so he knew.

When it's a human, you know, sharing words with you, as opposed to a synthetic voice, both are listening and breathing.

AB:: And breathing and listening are at the core of acting. As are trust and interdependence.

VD: Absolutely, yes.

AB: So, with all your ups and downs along the way, what would you wish could be done to better enable Blind artists and actors to be part of theatre in Canada?

VD: I would like Blind actors to be cast in roles where blindness does not define the character but happens to be a characteristic the actor possesses. Alternatively, it would be great if the lived experience of blindness would be considered a worthwhile story to tell and if Blind actors had access to more roles depicting this experience in a realistic and holistic way. I would like stories about blindness to portray the entire range of the human experience. It is not enough to cast a Blind actor in a role commonly associated with blindness: infantilized, helpless, having heightened sensory awareness. Or inspirational.

And I think that it isn't acceptable because these aren't the only ways to tell stories about blindness. We need to imagine a bigger world than that for the stories we want to tell, and how and who we want to tell them. And think about what Blind actors can bring to the craft. Be open to learning new ways to incorporate Blind actors in the process of making art and work with them to enable their success. Blindness is not the barrier. The lack of understanding, the absence of exploration, innovation, and collaboration, are the barriers.

AB: Let's finish with a question about the piece that you have submitted for the book, *Meditation on Snakes and Sightlessness*. What are you exploring here?

VD: This piece came out of one of the prompts we had during the rehearsal process for *Neither Here Nor There*. During one of our discussions, we were talking about the origin stories of Tiresias. One story really stuck with me, as it focused on snakes. The image kept returning to me, and I always feel in my writing – this has always been kind of a guiding principle – that when something won't leave me and my imagination alone, that means I need to write about it. And I am a person who doesn't even like snakes or – But then, on the converse of that, appreciating and understanding that snakes are magical, and they have such power and potency and significance in metaphor and in literature. So my aversion to snakes is what I'm trying to work through.

AB: Writing is both a creative act and some form of life processing?

VD: Yes. And it is very spiritual for me. And like life, it can be 'happily ever after,' and it can be messy and gritty, and I want to interrogate and navigate it all.

AB: Good thing you're an artist.

A Meditation on Snakes and Sightlessness

Vivi Dabee

Have you ever been asked, 'If you were a non-human animal, what animal would you be?' Have you ever thought about it? I know the question seems like a frivolous one. The type of question you would read in a quiz from a magazine or ask someone at a party to quickly analyze their personality. On the surface, this appears to be the purpose of asking such a question, the answer providing immediate insight into who the interlocutor is – a creature who is either warm and cuddly or cruel and vicious.

Well, I have been asked this question and I have given it careful consideration. It was a difficult choice, as I feel an affinity with many animals.

For a time, I felt that I mostly identified with an elephant. One reason for this is that elephants have matriarchal societies, and I have always been drawn to, surrounded by, and sought out strong women as supporters and guides. Elephants are found on the continents of Africa and Asia, which honours both parts of my ancestry. In addition, to think of myself in comparison to such an imposing species amused me as an ironic study in contrast, considering my stature. I then thought that the wolf best suited me. Wolves are social creatures, and like them, I feel most at ease when I am surrounded by my pack of family and friends. Finally, I decided that the dolphin was the most appropriate animal for me. They are joyful, friendly, fun, and flirtatious, qualities that I possess, and that most aptly describe me. Dolphins are also sensual creatures. Need I say more? On a more practical level, they rely upon sound to both communicate and navigate. I pondered this question again recently and was surprised to find where my musings led me this time.

It occurred to me that being Blind, I was particularly aligned with the snake – a thing of beauty that is feared. You are attracted to it, want to touch and hold it. It intrigues you because you do not fully understand it or how it moves through the world – sensing rather than seeing and using its entire body to explore its surroundings. It is not like other creatures you have encountered. If you get too close to it, it could strike you. Then what? Fill you full of venom. Or perhaps swallow you whole.

This is how it can feel in the wild world of love and romance. Blindness to a potential partner is venom, the kiss of death to a romantic relationship.

At first, you may be a curiosity, an exotic creature in the wild. People cannot help but be drawn in by your charm, your mystique, your beauty, and how smoothly you seem to live in this new skin you have adopted. But that is the nature of the snake, to shed its old skin and don a new one, is it not? Those of us who become Blind undergo a similar transformation. This metamorphosis, however, remains irreconcilable. We share a kinship with – yet are estranged from – our fellow humans. Despite undergoing the process of reacquainting ourselves with our now sightless bodies and adapting to a new way of being, traces of the creatures we once were linger inside us. As with the ouroboros, we must find a way to begin again after the life we have known has ended. Exposing ourselves to the world in a new way, we use our bodies to absorb knowledge and to feel for a connection with someone who will see us in our wholeness. Some of us are able to traverse this apparent species divide between the Blind and the sighted and find the love we seek. Others are not as fortunate and are either approached with caution or are fled from in fear.

There are those who, though they may be attracted to you, will not even approach you. As if to do so would fatally harm them – I promise I will not bite unless you want me to. You are poisonous, and contact with you would be deadly. How dare you confront them with their mortality – with the realization that the body is not eternal, is imperfect and susceptible to illness. How dare you force them to confront their worst fear – that they too may one day lose their sight and be plunged into darkness? Most important, how dare you deny them the possibility of affirmation by refusing to reflect what they most desire to see – the appraisal and approval of one they have chosen and deemed worthy of their affection. Woe to those of us who do not follow this carefully choreographed mating dance. We are left to experience a sense of loneliness that feels like death, and like Medusa we are transformed into abhorrent creatures without cause.

A tragic tale indeed. Medusa was the most beautiful of the Gorgon sisters and a devotee of the virgin goddess Athena. She was pursued and later raped by Poseidon because she would not yield to his sexual advances as she worshipped at Athena's temple. Outraged at the desecration of her sanctuary, Athena took vengeance upon the victim rather than the perpetrator of this crime and transformed Medusa into a reviled reptilian creature. However, Medusa was crowned with – not cursed by – serpents, as the story would lead you to believe, and attained the gift of chthonic wisdom. In the end, Perseus murdered her because she did not see as others did. Her gaze was not one of affirmation. It was not a gaze that submitted to protecting the fragile male ego. It did not perpetuate the myth that worthiness could be sought and found in the reflection of another's eyes. It did not grant the unspoken wish to be seen and chosen communicated in the exchange of glances that says, 'Yes, I see you. I see you the way you see yourself. I see you the way you want me to see you. I see you the way you want to be seen.' Instead, Medusa's gaze was one of defiance that presented a challenge to Perseus. A challenge for him to behold and acknowledge the sacred feminine and to recognize Medusa as an equal. How could he treat her as an equal when he feared her? Similarly, how can I be seen as an equal if I am feared? If my blindness is feared? If the myths perpetuated about blindness are those of difference and dependency? I am Blind, but I am not broken. Do not be afraid. Handle me with care, the way you would a snake or any creature you admire, respect, and love.

Garden Knows

JD Derbyshire

JD was a non-binary working-class artist, a self-described 'Queerdo' and a parent. They worked across forms including theatre, film, stand-up comedy, and published a novel at age sixty-one. Their work was fuelled by their commitment to accessibility and challenging the saneism and ableism in mainstream theatre practices. In this essay, they imagine a conversation with Disability Arts maverick Geoff McMurchy and unpack the challenges of bringing crip-art practices into integrated collaborations. Included is an excerpt from *Certified*, their one-person show.

His ashes are scattered in a backyard garden bed where the tulips are just popping up. It's been eight years since he died, so who knows if any of the salt and minerals and bits of his skeleton are even there anymore. It's likely that most of it has been washed away by the West Coast rains or sucked up from previous seasons of tulips to strengthen their stalks or brighten their bloom, or maybe it's been carried away by darker-hearted squirrels with a penchant for the occult. Whatever remains of his remains, I can hear what he would say about me coming here to talk to him: 'Ridiculous!'

His obituary in the *Globe and Mail* described him as Geoff McMurchy, a man who blazed a trail for Disability Arts. I believe he forged that wheelchair-accessible trail with his sometimes hot and spicy fiery opinions, but they don't mention that. They do say he was always an artist, and at twenty-one an accident cracked him into living life as a quadriplegic. They say that differently too, but so it goes.

According to the *Globe and Mail*, he lived the rest of his life making art, supporting other artists with disabilities, and trying to advance ideas of what Disability Arts could be. True, but I'm here to talk to those parts of him they don't mention in his obituary.

The way he could come across as an asshole sometimes and not really give a shit about what people thought of him – his slightly irritated directness, his salty almost-surety, his audacious juggling of blunt kindness, his dark humour, his sadness that squeezed him so tight sometimes it made him laugh, his refusal to live life as a victim, and how he would call me out if I leaned too far into that powerless position. I pull my lawn chair closer to the garden bed to talk to those little bits of Geoff I miss the most, those little bits I hope some mad squirrel hasn't carried away yet.

My friend, I'm struggling with two Disability Arts projects, and I really don't know who to talk to. One is a project I can't seem to support another artist's needs in, and one is a project I can't seem to support my own needs in. This seems to happen whenever disability theatre practices merge into mainstream theatre practices. Why is it that the theatre-making machine often needs to smash up differences and hide them in a recognizable package of basically the same old same old?

I hear myself explaining this to Geoff and getting all worked up about how integration just isn't good enough. If he was still alive, we'd likely be sitting on the patio outside his basement suite and looking at this same garden bed with the spring-shy tulips. I can see him listening deeply and then inhaling deeply on a joint. He'd exhale and then, with a sly smile, say, 'What did you expect?'

And Then We Would Laugh

What's true is that after his first gruff response, he'd often tell me it was important to say what I thought even if the response wasn't favourable, even if no one else agreed. He would tell me to back off the personal and say what I had experienced or what I needed. He would tell me I'd bitched enough, and it was time to get down what I thought. So, here's what I promised Geoff that I would tell you: opinions, my opinions, surfaced from decades of doing this work – worth something, according to a pile of dirt I had a conversation with last spring.

I am an artist who lives and works with disabilities. I also went back to school twelve years ago and got a master's in Inclusive Design. I was invited into the program without an undergrad degree because of my 'lived experience.' What a ride, but that's another story for another day. All I can say for now is that when one is bestowed with a title – in this case a paltry MDES – I notice that I become entitled. Entitled to be invited into conversations inside arts institutions and organizations that may not have thought I had much to say before those four little letters lined up behind my name. Now I make part of my living designing processes in practice and production for other artists with disabilities. One size fits one. I have been consulting for many years with an artist who wants to direct theatre, an artist who happens to have an intellectual disability to go along with his other talents of writing, painting, filmmaking, and acting. As the project he's directing nears production, it is clear we have lost the intention to support his unique aesthetic. It has become about answering to the vision of others who have moved things in the direction of what interests them. While I understand there is no malicious intent in moving toward what interests the other professional non-disabled actors and artists involved in the production, there is a fundamental disregard for Disability Arts and what we said we were trying to do.

    I tried to chirp in about the ways people take over this artist's work without realizing what they're doing. People push back against this idea; after all, they are here to 'help' this artist with a disability. This is an age-old problem in disability theatre – able-bodied, able-minded professionals who sign on to help and end up making it look like something that already exists, instead of supporting the new form and aesthetic it could be. I'm heartbroken because this wasn't just some experiment. It came about because this artist repeatedly expressed his hurt about previous projects. He was acutely aware of when his words or ideas were taken from him and moulded in ways he didn't agree with. He had the experience of several successful integrated projects, yet he was not given the opportunity to be in charge of his own work. That's what I believed we were trying to do. We were trying to make work inside these questions: What would it look like if we followed this artist's vision all the way through? How could we support this? How could we centre his care and protect his aesthetic as we moved through the various parts of the theatre production machine? What if it doesn't make sense? How do we keep our focus on developing him as a writer/director? How can we trust that his aesthetic will be interesting to others? How can we all remember that these questions are at the heart of what we mean by centring an artist with a disability?

I think the creative team believes they are all equal as creators, not unlike other collaborative projects they've worked on. This is not true in this particular Dis Arts project. We are here to answer to this artist, to develop this artist as a director. We wouldn't be here without this artist. We are all benefiting from this Disability Arts–funded project. We said we were here to realize this artist's vision, and that's it. We said we understood this from the start. Everything we offer should be in support of that. There is a fundamental distrust in the director/writer's vision.

Everyone has 'better' ideas.

This Is Ableism. Mine and Theirs. How Do We Talk About That?

The second project I came to talk to the tulips about has to do with my own work.

It is with a necessary humility and a reluctant sorrow that I recently called off an upcoming workshop and imminent production of a play I've been working on for three years. In the making and performing of *Certified*, an award-winning show, where I turn the audience into a mental health review board to determine my current state of sanity, I paid a big price for bringing the show into mainstream theatre spaces. The combination of what the show deals with, my unresolved issues with the saneist and ableist nature of theatre-making, and an inability to keep my nervous system regulated while doing the work has led me to making this decision. Once my nervous system is fired up (fancy psychopathology words: *deregulated*), it takes a long time for me to regulate again, especially inside the long hours and many voices found in workshops, rehearsals, and performances. I have now come to realize that I was in a state of perpetual hyperarousal for a few years, creating and then touring this show. I was unable to reset my nervous system and walked through the world unable to get any insulation back on my wires. I was in a continuous state of shock. My therapist has suggested that I'm feeling all this now because I may be healing some of my traumatic injuries. It is not without some horror that I grapple with the thought that I may want calm and ease more than I want to be making theatre.

Now, when I say I may want calm and ease more than making theatre, I mean making theatre in the way it's always been made. I don't think it's sustainable for anybody, or the price is too great, or we ask too much of artists. Offer us your emotions and vulnerabilities, dear artist, but don't disturb the short time frame we have to get this up and done; don't ask for anything – especially time to take care of yourself. That's why we call it self-care – it's your job. And here I will risk quoting another dead white guy because it so succinctly explains why so many of us got into theatre in the first place.

I was perplexed as to what the usefulness of any of the arts might be, with the possible exception of interior decoration. The most positive notion I could come up with was what I call the canary-in-the-coal-mine theory of the arts. This theory argues that artists are useful to society because they are so sensitive. They are super-sensitive. They keel over like canaries in coal mines filled with poison gas, long before more robust types realize that any danger is there.

Geoff would not have hesitated in telling me that I was once again being SUPERSENSITIVE. So it goes.

The tulips even nodded in agreement that day.

I seldom bring up most of my 'supersensitivities' in mainstream workshops or rehearsal rooms. This is an easy practice to fall into with invisible disabilities. A word about one of mine: I am a voice hearer. I say I have voices in my head, but that's just to remind myself that they are made up. In fact, they come at me from the outside, loud and discordant and mean. Essentially, I am in a room full of screaming people all the time. They vary in volume and content from day to day, but they're always there. Whenever I'm working with other people, I am also working to sort their voices through 'my' voices. Ironically, it's why I'm such a good listener.

(Sometimes.) In situations of go, go, go … or let's say making and performing theatre … the constant firing of adrenaline turns the volume of the voices up and increases the nastiness of the content. This ups the fear for me that something the voices are saying will leak out into the room or that I will raise my voice when talking to you, literally just to hear myself think. This constant noise can also manifest in pressured speech, where I repeat ideas and overwhelm others. I put so much effort into masking what's going on for me, essentially the labour of appearing normal, while simultaneously trying to pay attention to everything that's going on that I often exhaust myself. When these things happen, they are often noted as overreactions by more regulated minds. And then I have the added labour of needing to explain myself.

I don't talk about this a lot, because the last thing I want is your pity. If I do tell you, what I want is your understanding. But it's a big ask, wanting someone to understand something they've likely never experienced. So usually, if I reveal at all, I am given a kind of understanding that's a near cousin to pity. You know: 'That must be really difficult for you.' Followed by a few days of overaccommodation. You know, the well-intentioned 'Hey, how are you doing? Are you okay? Do you need a break?' And then the disability disappears again, cloaked in a magic self-care cape, once more invisible. So, most of the time I am caught out pretending I don't have this disability, keeping my expectations of myself and what I am capable of extraordinarily high and impossible to meet 100 per cent of the time.

The truth is clear. Sometimes, because of my disabilities, I don't play well with others. And maybe I really couldn't know this before because I'm healing now and finally learning to accept myself as I am, even when others can't. This, combined with that drive of me and everyone around me trying to make a 'good' show in the always limited time we have, is not something I enjoy anymore. In the past I have described this feeling of hyperarousal and vigilance as the feeling of being alive. I don't know what I'm going to feel without it. Hopefully, not the feeling of being dead. I guess I won't know for sure until my ashes are as scattered as Geoff's.

One thing seems certain – the theatre-making machine isn't going to change any time soon, so I will change directions.

This Is Saneism, Mine and Yours. How Do We Talk About That?

A light rain starts to fall in the backyard in Victoria, and I close my notebook, grateful that the sky can cry when I can't. I know because of Geoff's mentorship that I will go home and try to make some sense of it all. Not to be agreed with, but maybe to keep trying to get some words out there that might help someone else feel less crazy or maybe give someone else a thought they hadn't had before.

At some point, I hope I can integrate all this 'lived experience' and continue to help develop artists with disabilities and really understand what that means. I also hope I can continue to accommodate myself inside my own creativity. Right now, however, I feel a decades-old fatigue settling over me, because we will never know how my friend with an intellectual disability truly envisioned his work, because we took it from him. And I might not be able to realize a play I believed in, because I can't figure out how to include myself and some of my behaviours that are socially unacceptable to others.

All is not lost. Mine has been a life of adaptation; it's what artists with disabilities do. My writing practice has become something I have learned to run through a different, calmer route of my mind. I guess I can answer to my own rhythms easier. I guess the focus required keeps the voices partying in another room. Noisy neighbours I would prefer not to have, but they don't make life unlivable. One-on-one collaborations and slower, longer development periods with people I've known a long time also seem to help. I'll keep trying to talk with and listen to others about all this messy shit when I have some insulation on the wires again. I will even go so far as to continue visiting with scattered elders like Geoff McMurchy, who went before me, and too fucking soon if you ask me.

Geoff McMurchy, whose obituary says he was relentless in his Disability Arts and Justice work, accomplished a lot. It's true, google him. But he wasn't an idealist. He seemed satisfied with the little wins that saying uncomfortable things brought and not giving too much of a shit about the big changes that might never come. Maybe it was the joints he smoked at night; maybe it was this backyard garden he planned and had planted with the help of friends; maybe it was that he always had his own art practice going, making sculptures and installations from found objects. Whatever it was, his ability to hold dissatisfaction in his heart, without giving up, and his apparent acceptance of 'Right now it's like this and I care, but not too much,' is something I wish I had.

When I went back last week to the garden beds, now fully in bloom like a private little Pride parade, tulips in every colour and shape, bopping along in the wind, a particularly bright orange parrot tulip spoke to me. This was right after I offered this bold, ruffle-headed wonder of a tulip a chance to suck back on a joint. The tulip, speaking in Geoff's gravely Alberta-influenced drawl, coughed and said, "God, I miss pot."

God, I miss Geoff.

He really was the most driven stoner I've ever known and the most cynically caring artist/activist I've yet to meet. I'm still not sure whether getting all these thoughts down and out is a good idea, but for now I choose to place my trust in a stoned flower – all I have left of a wise and often irritable old friend.

May the conversations continue.

May the work continue.

With gratitude to Paula Jardine, one of Geoff's besties and an upstairs neighbour who lets me come and get her flowers high whenever I want.

Excerpt from *Certified*
JD Derbyshire

17. Chronic Female

It could have been so much worse. I was living beyond the lifetimes of Virginia Woolf, Zelda Fitzgerald, Frances Farmer, Sylvia Plath, Janet Frame, or T. S. Eliot's wife – what was her name? Oh well, the point being, spare the wife, spoil the poet. And who could keep track of the hordes of Freudian-slip-wearing women deemed hysterical for the mad act of yelling the truth of their experiences. I didn't put rocks into my pockets and walk into a river, I wasn't sent away and locked up for good, I wasn't lobotomized, I didn't stick my head into a gas oven, I wasn't shocked repeatedly into forgetting myself. If it had been even thirty years earlier, I might have been committed long-term to the Riverview psychiatric facility in Coquitlam, B.C. The building where women were kept was called the Female Chronic Unit. I've seen pictures where they carry the drugs up to the women in ice cream buckets. The Female Chronic Unit. I mean, they wouldn't have been wrong. I am a long-suffering woman, a female, chronic unit. FCU. Fuck you.

18. In and Out

Where is my gratitude? I was allowed to leave the hospital. Every time I left, I felt like I was wearing a pharmaceutical straitjacket that no one could see. Every time I left, I felt like I was walking on carpet-covered sand, sinking down with every step but not quite deep enough to keep from moving on.

In downpours that slicked back my hair and dripped off my nose, I'd walk to the Lions Gate Bridge. The rain melted me like sugar, inviting me to completely disappear. I was frightened, flattened out in that place between not wanting to live and not wanting to die. I would walk to the bridge every night for months sometimes. On the nights I felt certain I was supposed to die, I'd lean over the bridge railing far enough to see the grey turbid waters below. And every time I did that, something would pull me back. It felt like a hand grabbed my belt to yank me away from the edge. When I'd turn around, there was no one there. Sometimes there was a seagull, and the seagull would say, 'Your presence will be required at a later date.' On those nights I'd walk myself to St. Paul's Hospital. They'd certify me to protect me from me, adjust my meds, and then after three or four weeks send me on my way. I'd be back at the psych ward every six months or so for five years, and then that period of my life ended. What the fuck happened? Thanks for asking.

19. Margot Kidder

JD: *(goes back and forth in a conversation between two teenagers on the bus)* Well, one day, I heard on the bus that /Margot Kidder is coming to town. /Who's Margot Kidder? /You know Margot Kidder, Lois Lane – Superman's girlfriend. But the really old Superman, like your grandpa's Superman. He's dead now /Oh /And she's bipolar /She likes to make love to both men and woman in really cold climates? /No, she's crazy, but she doesn't take any drugs anymore. /Weird /Right? /Margot Kidder is the keynote speaker at some orthomolecular psychology conference. I go. Lois Lane speaks: 'Bipolar? Bullshit. Nutritional deficiencies. Mental illness? Physical illness. Head not separate from body. Biochemical imbalance. Not chemical imbalance. Too many drugs. Not enough vitamins, minerals, amino acids. It's a physical fucking illness.'

I experience my first tickle of hope in 700,432,000 seconds, but who's counting. And then I imagine Lois Lane flying toward me in her perfectly pressed linen suit. She must be wearing Superman's old red tights underneath. Lois Lane scoops me up into her arms, flies me out of Hotel Vancouver, up and over downtown, and lands me in a swish naturopath's clinic on Broadway. In about half the time it would take on transit, and I flew for free. Thank you, Lois Lane. I quickly discover I don't have the kind of money it would take for the alternative treatments I would require. The government will pay for drugs and hospital stays, but not vitamins, minerals, or therapy. But fear not, Lois Lane is here. She signs a blank cheque to cover everything I'll need. Now that's Super Mam! I come out of my daydream in time to see the real Margot Kidder signing autographs for a long line of orthomolecular psychologists I will never be able to afford to see.

I leave and go to where all the poor people go to learn – the library. I read what little I can find on alternative treatments for mental illnesses. It's then I learn that some psychiatric medications can actually cause suicidal ideation. I find an organization called the Icarus Project. They have all this information on how to make your way through life with mental illness, what psychiatric pharmaceuticals can and cannot do, how to safely get off as many of your drugs as possible. I feel like I'm in the library watching psychiatric porn. I download their free e-book. I feel crazy, but I begin to slowly wean myself off my meds and take as many vitamins and minerals as I can afford. I take a job at Starbucks. It's the only job I can get. My resumé's been a bit spotty in the last few years.

JD: *(converses with a customer)* Could I get a half fat, no foam, extra-hot cappuccino, tall /You know caffeine does not give you energy. It stimulates your nervous system and that's not energy, that's stress /Make it a Venti, bitch.

20. The Online Gang

I don't know what I'm doing or where this is all going to go. I can't imagine living with the voices again and I can't imagine staying alive on all those pills. Who put the ills in pills? I don't have anyone to talk to about all of this. Luckily, I find this online support group: Voice Hearers of Britain. I get three chat room pals who live with voices like me: Schizo Susie, Cray Cray Craig, and One Chip Short. I sign on as Shit House Rat. They advise. I listen.

JD: *(alternates between three English accents)* All right, the voices, treat them like the bullies they are, tell them to fuck off. /Yeah, but if they don't, you need to learn to negotiate breaks – I need to focus for an hour, then you can have five loud minutes. /Yes, love, but there's lots of practical things; listen to lots of music, drink lots of water, take your vitamins, sleep eight regular hours, exercise, eat all the right foods, no additives, preservatives, colours, nothing fried, no sugar. No doughnuts for you, darling. No caffeine, no alcohol or drugs. No smoking. /Pause when agitated or doubtful. Write, write, write, write. /Avoid toxic people and conversations. /Avoid avoiding. Participate. /Pray. Meditate. Don't talk too much about poo or pee or sex. /Know your limits. /Avoid getting overstimulated./ Try new activities, make friends. /Keep your world small, /but not too small. /Be on the lookout for distorted thinking. /Trust your gut, learn to follow your own instincts. /Be positive, /be cautious / but take emotional risks. Work but not too much. /Stay present. /Don't futurize. Don't pasteurize. /Learn to love your own uniquely beautiful mind. /And get out of the bloody house.

Access and Intimacy

In Conversation with Andrew Gurza

Writer and sex and Disability consultant Andrew Gurza is the creator of the hit podcast *Disability After Dark*. He's designed sex toys for people with limited hand function, appeared in queer porn, and written a book called *Notes from a Queer Cripple*. In conversation with Debbie Patterson, Andrew discusses their experiences as a queer disabled person in the Canadian theatre space, and what it was like co-creating their award-winning show *Access Me*. Included is an excerpt from its 2023 production.

Debbie Patterson: Can you tell me about your experience of working on *Access Me*, and the other experiences you had had with theatre prior to that work?

Andrew Gurza: Cool. Prior to *Access Me*, I'd been an audience member, but I'd never had any experience in theatre. I was very naive going into the process. I thought, when I sat down with our lovely crew at the first meeting we had, that this will be done in six months. I truly didn't understand the process. I didn't realize the barriers, especially in a Canadian context, of getting funding to do a show.

DP: Yeah, there's a huge amount of resources that go into making a play.

AG: I just was so naive. I didn't realize the work that went into making a show, and so I was immediately humbled when we started doing it – like, oh, wow.

DP: Were you familiar with the other creators? Had you ever had other opportunities to work with other gay wheelchair users on other projects or in other contexts?

AG: I kind of knew who Ken [Harrower] was, but I didn't know who Frank [Hull] was. I knew about Ken through his other acting work, because people would tag me in his stuff and I remember being kind of jealous of him, because I was like, 'Well, this guy's doing what I want to do.' But no, I had never been in a room with other queer, Disabled men like that.

DP: What was the process like for you? Did you learn anything surprising or unexpected?

AG: Through the whole experience, I think I learned that each of our experiences is different, each of our experiences is valid, and we each deserve a space. I remember coming into it – not that I wanted to sound pompous – but I remember coming into it thinking, 'I'm gonna be the star. I'm the young one. I'm the famous one,' which is kind of a douchey thing to do – come in being the Beyoncé of the group, which is not very nice. So I really was humbled by the work. After that first summer where we kind of sat in the Cahoots Theatre space and created it, we got the bones of it up and running. And to be humbled by 'Oh my God, I have to remember this. I have to hit a mark. And what if I suck? And what if I'm not good at it? And what do I not know?' So I was really humbled by how much work it is to do this.

DP: Are you interested in doing more theatre?

AG: You know, funnily enough, I just wrote a book and I would love to stage my book as a play. Because a lot of the stuff I talk about in the play I talk about in the book, but in a much deeper sort of way. So I would love to do it again. I think that if we did *Access Me* again, I would love to have more money to stage it bigger than we did. I would want the benefactors to give us a million dollars, or a big sum of money, to make it bigger than what it was. But at the same time, I liked the smallness of what we were doing. I like the community aspect of what we did, for those eight weeks, it was so nice to have that camaraderie. I don't think I would give that back for any kind of fame or to do it on a bigger scale. That was so transformative for me, for all of us who worked on that show; we'll have that show forever, and I would never give that up for anything.

DP: I want to talk specifically about the intimacy with the audience. Would you describe the intimacy experiment?

AG: The intimacy experiment was a part of the show where I would take a member of the audience and say, 'Okay, now you're gonna pretend like you're my attendant. You have to get me up in the morning, and I want you to say good morning.' So they would say good morning. And I would say, 'Great. You said that really coldly and impersonally, like my care staff does. Great. Thank you.' And I would say, 'Now I want you to pretend like we're lovers and say good morning again.' So they would, they would say, 'Good morning, Andrew.' And I would say, 'Oh, that's, you know, you're almost there, but you're not really there yet.' And then I would get them to do that again, making them increase how sexy it was. And then we go from 'Good morning' to 'Now it's time for you to get me up,' or 'Now it's time for you to help me have a shower. And so, if you were gonna shower me, pretend like you're my attendant, I'm gonna give you my arm.' And I would give the audience member my arm, and I would say, 'Now, scrub up my arm like you're my attendant.' They would do it pretty efficiently. And I would say, 'That's okay, good, good.' And then I would say something like, 'Okay, now we're lovers, and we're in the shower together. How would you stroke my arm?'

And the game went on and on like that. And I think the last question was 'Now you're gonna put me to bed, and I want you to say good night to me like you're my attendant.' And they would say, 'Good night, Andrew.' And then I would say, 'Okay, now we're lovers. Say goodnight to me.' And every time they would say goodnight for this one, I would say, 'Oh, you're not quite there yet. Do it again.' And I would make them be really sensual with me to show that it is possible to have an intimate relationship with a Disabled person. I think in that last one, one of my prompts was 'Would you also give me a kiss?' Or 'Would you whisper something sexy in my ear.' And so, just to play with them and show that I'm also a human being who has a sexuality.

DP: What I loved about it was it was so playful, and it kind of showed how sexiness is so much in playfulness. Our idea of sexy is so aesthetic, so visual, but if you actually engage with someone in a playful way, it's supersexy and it has nothing to do with what their body looks like.

AG: Nothing at all. I think what I appreciated about doing that scene at the beginning is a lot of the play was really heavy. Frank's and Ken's characters were playful too, but they were unpacking abuse. My character didn't deal with that, so I got to make jokes. And so those scenes where I'm playing with the audience are really fun because I don't have to dig deep, as the other two did.

DP: Well, you dig deep in a different way. You dig deep into delight. How was it being touched by strangers every day, or approaching strangers to engage with you in that game of intimacy?

AG: It never scared me, because that's where my Beyoncéness – that's where my 'I'm a star' thing – came in really well, because I could tell myself, 'You're not Andrew right now. You're this character of Andrew.' So I was not really scared of it. I think the scarier interaction was at the end.

DP: The hookup scene with Ginger Beef. Can you talk a little bit about who Ginger Beef was?

AG: Ginger Beef? He was an amalgamation of guys who I had chatted with on the apps for a quick 3 a.m. hookup when I was younger. And so Ginger Beef is present throughout the whole play. There's a scene where my character is texting Ginger Beef, and he's texting back, trying to arrange a hookup. And then at the end, I would ask an audience member to play Ginger Beef. He comes over, and the implication is that we are going to have sex. And it was so fun, because every night that we did it, Ginger Beef was a different person. I have to pick a Ginger Beef from the audience, and I have to get them to take my shirt off and then hoist me in the sling, in the lift.

I wasn't scared of that, but you never know how an audience is going to perceive jumping into a real thing with a Disabled person. They have to actually put me in a Hoyer lift and lift me up, take off my shirt and touch me, and so you never know how someone's going to react to that, right? But I loved doing that kind of stuff because it forced the audience to confront their own discomfort around disability in a way that wasn't shaming them, that didn't put them down, that didn't scream at them, that didn't make them feel inadequate, or that they'd somehow failed. It said, 'We're all in this together, and we just want to play with you.'

We would do a game where we went around the audience and picked somebody who would have to ask a question. That was so fun, because you could see them get uncomfortable. And the minute one of us would make a joke about it, you see them relax a bit, and recognize, 'Oh, these people have sexual desires too. They're not so scary.'

DP: Can you remember any of the questions we made the audience ask you?

AG: Questions like, Can you go to the bathroom by yourself? Do I have to kneel down to talk to you? If I wanted to have sex with you, how would I do it? Or if I wanted to get into it with you, how would I do it? Does it work? Or how do you masturbate?

What I loved was those are real questions that all three of us had been posed at some point in our sexuality journeys. Those are real questions, and our answers were playful. But it was really fun to watch the audience grapple with feeling like 'I can't ask that.' They were so lovely, but they were uncomfortable, they didn't want to offend us, and I think that speaks to how embedded ableism is in our culture, that we got to bring that out for an audience, for them to see it.

DP: Non-Disabled people have internalized their own ableism, and it limits them in how they live their lives. And so I really think seeing that show with you three Disabled guys claiming your sexuality so brazenly gave a lot of people licence to be more at home in their own bodies and their own sexualities.

AG: Yeah, I hope so. The play allowed us to be unabashedly queer and talk about fucking and talk about hooking up and talk about fantasizing about fucking the guy in the bathroom. That was part of the play for us. I remember when they did the news piece for us, they wouldn't talk about it. They couldn't, frankly, say the show is about sexuality. One piece said something like 'The show is about accessibility in the village.' And we were like, 'Well, no, no.' They couldn't really get to what the truth of the play was, because to say what it is would be too scary. So I think it was groundbreaking.

When we did a couple run-throughs of our first workshop, I remember prominent Toronto theatre people said, 'Oh, the show is really sexual … Why is it so sexual?'

Because it has to be, because if [we] don't shove it in your face, you're not going to look at us. If you did a play about queer, able-bodied sex, nobody would stop you, right? Why can't we say cock and balls and why can't we do all the same stuff? And why are we judged so much more harshly for it?

DP: Even just expressing horniness is an anti-ableist expression, you know? Ableism expects us to sort of suppress and deny all our physical needs, all our messy humanness, right? So denying your horniness is ableist.

AG: Ken wanted to call the play *Horny!* with an exclamation point.

I kind of wish we had advertised to, like, the gay male sex clubs in Toronto and said, 'Come sit, watch this for an hour.' So that it would get into the bones of the community we were talking about. Because so much of what each of us said was 'I want to be included in all the debauchery that happens on Church Street Friday nights. I can't be included in that.' I wish we could have gone to a club here in Toronto called the Black Eagle, and there's a club called Flash and Cruise and Tangos and all of the prominent clubs. If we couldn't go there, they could come to us.

I would have loved to have had, like a leather night production, like a drag night production. Yeah, if we ever stage it again, if we ever get the chance to do it one more time for a couple weeks, I would die to have nights themed around one of these for sex workers, or drag queens, for leather daddies, for lesbians, for the trans community – every facet of our community. We get a chance to sit with that, to realize that disability will touch all those spaces. If we do it again, that's my dream.

DP: That's so beautiful. And, when a non-Disabled audience member interacts with you sexually and just gets an opportunity to – As artists, it's our job to imagine things, right? We have good imaginations. And the general population, their imaginations are good, but they're not as good as ours. So they need some help to imagine what it would be like to have sex with a Disabled person. You were just giving them an opportunity to begin to imagine what that could be. And then to imagine their own sexuality in light of that. It expands their scope. It expands their idea of who they are. So if Andrew Gurza can be so hot with the limitations that your body presents to you, if you can be so fucking hot, then how can anyone say that their body's limitations get in the way of their sexuality?

AG: Oh, my goodness, Debbie Patterson just told me I was so hot and I don't know. I'm gonna be on cloud nine for the rest of the day. No, but I agree with you. I think it gives the audience a place to explore their discomfort safely. 'Oh, a Disabled person turns me on. What do I do about that?'

And it makes them look at their own ability level. And when that changes, and it will for all of us, if we're lucky enough, they get to look at that and think, 'Well, when I need this mobility aid, I can still get intimate with somebody and not have it be an issue.'

DP: What was the biggest benefit of the project to you, like financial, relational, interpersonal, personal growth? How do you feel like you benefitted from doing that work?

AG: Well, I benefitted financially. It was nice to have every summer [we workshopped the show], a couple thousand coming in for doing that, and knowing that it was through an arts grant so it couldn't be taken away from my disability support. That was great. And then, interpersonally, hearing the other stories of the other gentlemen in the show and realizing, 'Yeah, Andrew, your story is important. But it's not the only one here that has to be told.'

There were moments where all of us were like, 'I don't want to do this anymore. Fuck off. See you later. Goodbye, yeah, and like, thank goodness.' We all took a breather and came back in the room. But I really appreciate even that stuff, stuff where all three of us piss each other off, but we got out there every day when we finally staged it, whether it was a reading or a workshop or the final show. I think that especially when you're making accessible theatre, like we were, there are challenges you don't think about, right? Sometimes Andrew's bus wouldn't show up. Or, you know, one of us was feeling ill, or one of us couldn't get there on time. Dealing with all those things, as a Disabled team, it brings you together way more than you think it would. When you're ready to lop each other's heads off, you're still like, 'Oh, I'm here for you. Don't worry.'

DP: Yeah. I learned so much from that project, and especially around things like that. Because I had never collaborated in that way with someone with mental illness and recognizing that it's just an access need. You know that someone may be behaving in a way that you might judge harshly in other circumstances. Or you might judge them for that behaviour, but their access need is to not be judged. It's so valuable to not judge someone – it's a much better way to move forward.

AG: So many of us were vulnerable in the room. And I loved how once we got into a rhythm every morning, it was like, 'How are you, what are your access needs? How do we do what we do? What do you need?' And learning the other actors' needs, and my needs too. And also having attending care on site was, for me, transformative. It's like, 'Oh, wow, I don't have to worry if I need something. I really need something and someone is there for me.' To have an attendant ready to go made my whole comfort level around going and leaving the house for seven hours a day, for six weeks, feel okay. I felt like, 'Okay, we can do this because someone's there.'

I don't think most plays would understand the need for that. There's such a misconception in theatre that you have to do it all independently. You have to do it yourself. And this play said, 'Fuck that.'

DP: Yep. It was great. Do you often have opportunities to have attendant care with you when you're out in the world?

AG: Not unless I hire it, right? I'm going to Washington next week – I was asked to be on a big international board of Disabled folks. And so, for that, I had to hire my own staff and figure out ways to get them paid and explain to the people hiring me, 'Without them, I can't go to your thing.' And so, typically, if I'm just around my neighbourhood, I don't leave my house unless I've gone pee, I've had food, I have enough water with me, because I don't have the privilege of having care with me all the time, right? So having Jordan, who was our great 'friend-tendant' for most of the run, was fantastic.

I wish I could take him everywhere, because he was really fun. And also he was queer, so it was really fun to just have somebody I could completely talk to normally about my experience and about how I was feeling in the show, or about how I talked to this guy on Grindr and here's my feeling about all of this. It was really nice to have a comrade in that.

DP: Yeah, yeah. He was a perfect friend.

AG: Perfect.

DP: Do you want to talk about the process of developing the whole script? I wasn't involved the first year, and that was when you just got together and shared stories.

AG: Which I can't even believe. You've been so integral to the show. But that's right. It was all of us sitting in the room and writing, just spitballing stories. That was really the part I loved the most, one of my favourite parts of the whole thing, because we just got to voice our truth and voice our stories, even if the stories were slightly embellished or slightly moved around a bit. We got to share that. I think it's very rare that three queer Disabled people, period, get to sit around together and talk. No one ever says, 'Tell me about your sex life, tell me about your intimacy, tell me about things you like.' We don't get to share those stories face to face. So that first week was transformative. And I remember sharing those stories and thinking, 'Oh, this can't be a show. This won't be anything.' And then that exact thing I said, 'Oh, this won't be anything,' was in the show. Going back to the collaboration between non-Disabled and Disabled, it was really cool to see how Jonathan [Seinen, the director] and Brian [Postalian, the associate director] and everybody else, with so much light and love about our stories, turned them into, like, here's a moment, here's a moment, here's a moment. The playfulness they brought to things that are really hard stuff to talk about was great.

DP: How did your character develop through the storytelling? Do you have a sense of how that happened, or was it so slow and organic that you can't even describe it?

AG: I'm pretty sure we all knew that I was the young one. I think immediately Jonathan picked up on that and was, like, 'Let's play with that. Let's make him the hip, cool one,' because I was the one talking about apps on my phone. Ken and Frank were like, 'Oh yeah, back in the eighties, when we used to go to the bar.' So right away there was a very clear dichotomy, and I think Jonathan and Brian could see that. But also Ken and Frank were talking about a lot of heavy stuff in their pieces. I think my character really balanced that out and also reminded the audience that Ken and Frank are talking about years past, but we're all talking about the same themes in different times. Which tells the audience that these feelings around disability haven't gone away. This friction around disability and queer sex hasn't gone away, no matter what timeline we're in, right? And I think that was really cool.

And so, I don't think there was much to develop, because the direction was just 'Be yourselves as much as you want to be.' I don't think any of the three of us had huge direction to worry about, but we were guided very deftly by the team on how to turn those stories into a scene and how to turn that story into something accessible to the whole audience. I had no idea how to do that beforehand. I had no clue how to turn my story into something that somebody would want to watch.

DP: The whole final scene, the final movement of the play, took place in your bedroom. That was completely constructed; that wasn't a story from your past, that was imaginative.

AG: That was my dream bedroom and my dream moment, and not only was it constructed theatrically, but also it was physically constructed. We built the bedroom for me, and we painted a wall pink, because that's what the character wants to see. I remember when we walked into the theatre for the first time and saw the set, I was like, 'Oh my God, that's my bedroom.' In one of the scenes I talked about *The Phantom of the Opera*, and I talked about being a theatre kid, and about being a big nerd. So there's a poster of *The Phantom of the Opera*. There's the pink bedspread. What [the designers] did to bring that to life, and then also to bring disability to life! We had a Hoyer lift onstage. They did stuff to show the audience that this is all fantasy, and this is all play, but these are the real things that wheelchair users really have to do to have a sexual encounter. And that attention to detail was really cool.

DP: Was there anything that surprised you in the process of making the play?

AG: Yeah, it was pretty great the way everybody who worked on the show took time to really pay attention to everything we were saying. And I never thought in a million years that the stories we shared that summer at Cahoots over three days would turn into what it did.

DP: You talk about non-Disabled people saying no to themselves, in terms of their responsiveness to others. When do *you* say no to yourself? And why?

AG: Like, why do you deny yourself the chance to have pleasure? And do you do it because you're afraid? When it comes to disability, the answer is yes. What I love about our show is we knew they were afraid of us. We knew they were fucking scared of us, but we didn't approach them like, 'You're scared of me.' We said, 'Okay, let's play with this.' Yeah, that's the stuff I really enjoyed: to have the audience members be confronted with things you talk about colloquially every day but are now forced to think about from a disability lens. I love that!

Excerpt from *Access Me*
Boys in Chairs Collective

A buzz and a lighting change. At the rear of the performance space, curtains part to reveal a fully realistic yet stylized recreation of Andrew's bedroom at home in pink, complete with bed, Hoyer lift (to transfer him from his chair to his bed), and Phantom of the Opera *poster. He is looking hot, dressed for a date, in his wheelchair next to his bed. As he talks out loud to an imaginary Ginger Beef, his internal thoughts are expressed by a voice-over reviewing the situation.*

ANDREW: Hey.

(voice-over) Oh my God, he's actually here. Be cool. Take a breath. It'll be okay, it'll be fine. I mean it'll be great, right? Like, he's not a creep, right?

Come in.

(voice-over) Who is this guy? I mean, will he know what to do? Will he know how to take my pants off? What if I smell bad?

I'm glad you came over.

(voice-over) He doesn't want to be here – he probably feels obligated and then he'll resent me. What if I come too fast?

Can I get you anything?

(voice-over) That's so silly! I can't get him anything – he'll have to get it himself 'cause I'm Disabled.

Make yourself comfortable.

(voice-over) Oh no – what if I have an IBS attack; what if I shit myself right now? What if I have to pee? He can't do a cath. What if I can't come? Then he'll never come back, and we won't move in together and have nights bingeing Netflix, and we'll never choose the china pattern for the gift registry for our accessible kitchen, and get the house with the white picket fence, and a Hoyer lift in every room, and a fleet of accessible vans, and adopt our four kids – Thomas, Christina, Don, and Riley, the little scamp – and we won't sit on the veranda watching

our grandkids frolicking in the mist of the water sprinkler. Disability whyyyyy?! Disability whyyyyyyy?!

Andrew exits his room, moving quickly toward the audience.

> Why do I keep doing this? Still, I'm here, and I kind of want to try. *(addressing audience)* Tonight you've seen that we've cast some people in very special roles. I'm wondering if anybody from our very sexy audience would like to play my Ginger Beef tonight?

Andrew surveys the audience.

> Anyone?

When a volunteer steps forward ...

> Awesome! Can I ask you to come up here? There's something for you in my bag.

As they look into the bag hanging on the back of his chair, they find a ginger wig.

> Put it on.

Sometimes they're confused, thinking Andrew wants to wear the wig.

> Put it on *you*.

The audience member puts it on.

> That looks amazing! You are now Ginger Beef.

This often earns them a round of applause.

> I'm wondering, can I ask you to come with me into my bedroom? If you feel comfortable ...

They agree. Andrew and Ginger Beef turn toward the bedroom and casually stroll on in.

> So, how are you doing? What have you been up to tonight?

They answer.

Excerpt from *Access Me*

At a show?

They usually say yes. They arrive in Andrew's bedroom. He gives them a tour of sorts.

So, these are my stuffed animals, here's my *Phantom of the Opera* poster, and this is my Hoyer lift. Also, my friend is here –

He indicates the attendant that the audience met at the beginning of the show.

– as my 'friend-tendant' if we need them.

Awkward hellos between Ginger Beef and the 'friend-tendant.'

Would you like to hold my hand?

They agree.

I'm wondering if you would like to take off my shirt?

They say yes.

What you are going to do is lean me forward a little bit, and you're going to pull the shirt up over my head. Take my shoulders and pull.

This takes a while. Ginger Beef is usually a bit tentative, but Andrew is patient and affirming.

You're doing great … Nearly there … Pull harder!

The shirt is off.

Okay, great. Now, know what I want you to do? I want you to throw it across the room like we're going to make out. Passionately!

They throw the shirt.

I mean … could you do that one more time? It wasn't quite passionate enough. Just, like, throw it across the room really passionately. Okay, go!

They retrieve the shirt and throw it again. Passionately!

Yesss! So, these are my tattoos. Would you like to remove your shirt too? Maybe take it off passionately.

They rip off their shirt with reckless abandon and toss it aside. Or sometimes they don't.

Would you like to get into bed with me?

They say yes.

Okay. We're going to use this special machine. And I'm going to show you what to do.

Andrew has pre-set his sling on his torso. He directs Ginger Beef to retrieve the sling straps from under his thighs and behind his shoulders. He directs Ginger Beef to attach the sling straps to the Hoyer lift. This takes quite a while. It is intimate, awkward, funny, and tender. And hot. Once the straps are safely secured to the lift …

Okay, you're going to take the control thing from my 'friend-tendant' there and you're going to press 'up' all the way.

GINGER BEEF: All the way?

ANDREW: All the way.

Andrew rises in the Hoyer lift. Slowly. Very slowly. He looks at the audience.

Hey, everybody!

Once he is completely in the air …

Okay, this part of the show is private.

The curtain closes on Andrew and Ginger Beef.

Anybody Is an Artist

In Conversation with Niall McNeil

Acclaimed actor and playwright Niall McNeil has sustained a multidisciplinary practice across several decades. His formative years as an actor with Down Syndrome were spent at the Caravan Farm Theatre in Armstrong, British Columbia, which had a powerful influence on his work and world view. He is the co-writer of plays including the award-winning *Peter Panties* and the internationally toured *King Arthur's Night*. His intuitive and expressive use of the English language is part of his aesthetic, reflected below in his conversation with Debbie Patterson. Included is an excerpt from Niall's play *Beauty and the Beast: My Life*, first produced in March 2025 at the Cultch in Vancouver.

Debbie Patterson: Hey, Niall, I know you fairly well as a theatre maker, but could you tell me a little bit more about your arts practice in general?

Niall McNeil: My practice, sketching, painting, everybody can paint, make sketches, anything they want. It's not about you cannot or can do it: you can do it, I know you can. I'm hard of hearing. I can read ASL. I can read lips and I'm very good at having eye contact when somebody's talking to me. I don't look this way or that way. You look at the person you're talking to. Anybody has the ability. Anybody is an artist. And we all need a lot of support on a regular basis.

DP: You've worked on so many different projects. Can you talk a bit about where your ideas for projects come from?

NM: My open mind is the start with all different scripts. Let's say, *Peter Panties*: me and Marcus (Youssef) started creating. Marcus would have a phone and record everything I say, and it was on his phone until he gets home. He sits and he can play it back and forth until he's got it right, and he comes to me with the words. And the music, I sing on my phone. My practice is kind of, like with Marcus, so easy to listen to all of the person and my imagination.

I liked *Peter Pan*, not really Walt Disney. I like *Hook*, a film made in 1982 with Robin Williams. Robin Williams was in his forties or thirties. God knows where he is now.

DP: And after *Peter Panties*, you made *King Arthur's Night*, right?

NM: I'm inspired by King Arthur's story. We did King Arthur onstage with Jamie Long. He was our director. We don't need to … You can't look straight to the door, that's rude. Look at the director and listen to the director. If you don't listen to them, how can you do the play if you don't listen to him? People have disabilities, but they can listen. When I'm inspired, I write – it's on my phone or my tablet. I, Marcus, Veda (Hille), and Jamie: we co-write. Any time I have a song, I can speak it as a song. I record it and I give it to Veda. The same thing that we did with *Peter Panties*. And that's how you shape a script. One is write the script, then memorize the script. That means line by line of the script. Memorizing how you take it by heart.

DP: Did you know a lot about King Arthur's story before you started?

NM: I love research. I did a lot of research until, 'Hey, I think we can do it.' Because Lancelot has an affair with Guinevere. I don't like it, as King Arthur. We did a whole play. And music, hard-core rock 'n' roll. We dug into research, character research, how you meet the characters. The quest of the Holy Grail, it takes five nights and five days to get to the actual spot of God. Then my queen in *King Arthur's Night* got the Grail, put it in my backpack, and she carried it for five days and five nights and arrived back in Camelot. 'That's my dear, give it to the king, to King Arthur.' And it's kind of a secret package that Mordred cannot really see it.

Mordred tried to go take over my kingdom. I said, 'No, you can't have this kingdom. You might do something quite a bit stupid.' It is rude to take somebody's kingdom. Because I rule that kingdom and Mordred must be died.

DP: And there are goats! I really love the goats in *King Arthur's Night*. Can you talk a bit about where that idea came from?

NM: That idea came from when Mom was feeding the goats – dairy, oats, and hay. And that was before I go to school. Every day she would do that before I go to school. And one day I got an egg carton. I didn't know better. I was hitting the goat and I got butted like hard. I was screaming, and poor David Balser, he came running. Grabbed me up, locked the gate, and then I was okay. Mom had a job milking the goats. Because my song in *King Arthur's Night* 'mother, daddy, mother, daddy, baa baa,' it was just kind of hilarious. So we practised that. It was hard at first, but then it was so easy.

DP: There was a big cast for that show. And there was a mix of Disabled and non-Disabled actors in the show.

NM: Some of the actors were Matthew Tom-Wing, that was the Goatherd. There was Nathan, Lucy, Billy, and Amber. All four of them were goats. We had me, we have Matthew, we had Andrew and Tiffany. Four actors with Down syndrome and the rest were actors with no disabilities.

DP: What are you working on right now?

NM: The next work I've been working on is *Cowboy Tempest* in Toronto. It's been six or seven years. We've been making a lot of cuts and now we're coming down to the final moment. I first started to really collaborate with other people: *Do you like to participate in performance or are you more into play-writing a script and giving it to the actors?* Because a script isn't just writing, there's going to be a lot of cuts. The book of script and score: this one, Anton Lipovetsky made the score. Lucy McNulty and Anton made the book with me.

DP: What projects do you have coming up?

NM: I have a new idea about *Macbeth*. Livestream, live actors. Me and Marcus, our job is to interview them, saying, 'What is a bad host and what is a good host?' I want them to answer. It will have eleven songs and eleven underscores. And we will have a few garage bands. And there's another thing too: Malcolm is the son and heir. Is he a good friend or a bad friend? MacBeth is not a good friend. So that's a question I want them to answer. So it's like, we're going to have a livestream on the tablet doing the interviews and let them speak to their interview. Half interviews and half acting. It's going to have four swords. Not real swords.

Then there's *Beauty and the Beast*. In my scrotum up here *(points to his head and laughs)*, I mean my brain. I'm not taking Walt Disney, I'm taking my version of dancers with canvasses of my artwork. The back of a canvas will have handles and they can move it anywhere. And recordings are Veda singing, I'm not singing, and then there's drums and there's bass and there's violins. And there's all, like, music. And I sing poetry.

DP: Do you primarily work with other Disabled artists? Or does it matter to you?

NM: I like working along with somebody with all different disabilities. It's just like you, you're coming into the door. And if somebody can't really come in, like they're in a wheelchair, I let you in first, let the handicap person go first. I have to let them in first, not just me. You need to go first because of your wheelchair. I can walk, I can go in. But other people have disabilities that you can't see but you can hear. It's kind of like helping each other out.

And when you're working with somebody, it's not just me who is speaking, we all have to be able to speak too. And it's kind of like, their practice is, let them finish what their practice is. And doing a cue to cue rehearsal, do not make sounds, you can do anything, you can take photos, but don't make phone calls or look at your phone, you're supposed to focus. Pay attention.

DP: Is there anything other people should know about working with actors with Down syndrome?

NM: There are many actors with Down syndrome. Andre, Lewis, and Nick, and there's Dylan and there's me and there's Tiffany. There's Nick Chan. Everywhere. And Aaron Cunningham. Now I'm speaking for them. They make theatre too. And Aaron is such a good actor. He does the lead. People who have Down syndrome, you've got to listen to them, and if you don't listen to them, you're not participating. They can do more work, imagine they can. In the community, people with Down syndrome always participate in plays. You see people with Down syndrome in plays. Never look down, look up to them. When people look down on me, I'm sad, you can't really look down. That's not where Down syndrome is. And they can really – they can make people upset. Everybody who has Down syndrome can be in community, meeting new people like we saw today in the room.

Most people who have Down syndrome have challenges. Like I have hearing aids. And Gary, he has lots of episodes and he doesn't know who he is. He gets scared, he tries to blame everybody, but that's what his episodes are. I've known Gary since I was twenty or twenty-two. It's so hard for him to learn who people are. But he's getting better, he does meditation. And some other people have medical problems, including me.

DP: What do you think is the most important thing about making theatre?

NM: It's very important to love the people you work with, because when you work with someone you love, you work better with them. And if somebody is being rude, I'm not going to work with them. Don't be snobby, don't be hasty, just be listening. Be respectful.

DP: Thanks so much for this talk, Niall. Do you have any final thoughts?

NM: The last thing I'm going to say – I'm a visual artist and my practice is theatre. I'm a director, the fight choreographer. I do all different kinds of choreo: fight choreo, movement choreo. Everybody who has Down syndrome, they have their own practice and their own programs. I've got a lot more theatre going on and I work at Fresh Mart. My name is Niall Patrick McNeil Gillespie.

Excerpt from *Beauty and the Beast: My Life* (BBML)
Niall McNeil

My Life 5

Niall signs while performers speak this text.

> It is hard to be a writer. Patience to become one.
> To be a writer it is hard.
> How you going to be, nobody's perfect and my repetition.
> And that Christmases and two sides – my mom's side and my dad's side.

Ghost of Gaston

'Spooky Haunting Curtain Call' track plays. Insect buzz noises play. Evil Sister is walking in forest, sees tombstone. Evil Sister reaches her hand into the tombstone. Gaston smacks the hand. Then the Ghost of Gaston appears. The sound fades out.

GASTON: *(whispers)* Where's villagers? How much?

EVIL SISTER: Three.

GASTON: Go find them, bring them to me.

Evil Sister goes over the bridge and brings villagers back to Ghost of Gaston's tombstone.

GASTON: I just saw a ghost. I saw my brother.

VILLAGERS: I don't believe in ghosts.

EVIL SISTER: I need you to come. It was the Ghost of Gaston.

VILLAGERS: I don't believe you.

EVIL SISTER: You have to trust me. He told me to come get you and bring you with me.

VILLAGERS: I'm kinda busy.

EVIL SISTER: I'll take care of you.

VILLAGERS: OK.

The Villagers and Evil Sister go back through to the forest. They encounter bugs and swat them off. They arrive at the tombstone.

GASTON: *(to the Villagers)* The Beast killed me. Are you scared? Scaredy-cat!

VILLAGERS: *(shaking, scared)* No, we're not scared.

GASTON: We need to do something to defeat the Beast. You must kill the Beast.

VILLAGERS: No way. Says who?

GASTON: Says me. Kill the Beast.

VILLAGERS: *(chanting)* Kill the Beast! Kill the Beast! Kill the Beast! Kill the Beast!

GASTON: OK, OK, OK! Go now, kill the Beast. Then afterwards, drinks are on me.

Villagers agree and go to the castle.

EVIL SISTER: Here's the castle.

They ring the doorbell.

EVIL SISTER: Nobody's home.

Creaky door sounds. They are scared.

BEAST: What are you doing here?

EVIL SISTER: We're here to kill you. Kill the Beast! (chanting) Kill the Beast! Kill the Beast! Kill the Beast!

Excerpt from *Beauty and the Beast: My Life*

BEAST: That's enough. Fight to the death!

EVIL SISTER: Yep.

BEAST: Fine.

Angry Mob

They have a big fight.

SINGING:
>Mob is angry all the time, angry mob
>Mob is angry all the time, angry mob
>Let's kill the Beast
>Castle is haunted
>Throw the whisky
>Why is my daughter
>To find my daughter sitting danger
>Angry mob, mob is angry all the time
>
>I didn't do my daughter's in danger
>Angry mob, mob is angry all the time
>Knives pitchforks torches anger
>And the banks are made of marble
>And we'll open every door
>And we'll share those vaults of silver
>That the beast is sitting on
>Mob is angry all the time, angry mob
>
>Let's kill the Beast
>Castle is haunted
>Throw the whisky
>That's what you wanted

The Beast is defeated.

Beast Transforms

Niall places a gravestone by Beast's body. Belle mourns over Beast's body. Belle goes over his eyebrows, face, beard, full body, feet, legs, arms.

South, West, East

NIALL'S VOICE: *(in audio)*
Self, Swimming
 (Two drum beats.)
And this is what represents of
 (Drum beat.)
A heartbeat on this drum
 (Drum beat.)
And if maybe I decide about my life, about beauty and the beast, my life
Two beats in the heart, three beats
 (Five drum beats.)
You can hear your heart pumping
And military piano
 (Piano plays.)
And one day, I will not be here
That's only for BBML

The Beast itself is gone
And you know the Beast might be back
 (Drum beat.)
You can hear the drum
 (Drum beat and June's drum plays.)
And the Beast has got some wires to hook up to pull him up
And this time he will be a prince
 (Two drum beats.)
And this time, I'm not gonna speak
My drum is gonna speak overlapping piano and the drum
Military June

You can get louder, June
> (Instrumental break with piano, violin, drums, and Niall's drum.)

South, West, North, South, West, East
Vancouver, Kamloops

Five drum beats.

Beast is revived. Belle takes off his mask. The objects are released from the spell. They explore each other's bodies and dance. Belle hugs beast.

Beast Transforms Back into Prince

Belle and Beast dance into a tableau. Niall comes onstage and replaces Beast.

GUARD: *(out loud)* My lord, look at us. We're not objects no more. My lord.

BILLY: *(out loud)* My captain.

Everyone hugs. The cast links arms into a line downstage.

My Life 6: End of Play

Niall signs while performers speak this text.

> My life.
>
> First, it was my parents who got me in this world. And I was a little child until now I love to be here at Commercial Drive. And I can't remember the years. The past went. How many years, how was that being child for number years?
>
> I think I was a legend of myself: east and west and south, all altogether because we're equal. Equal means. There's no leaders. It is. That means you're equal to yourself. Tea time at 6:30 and after, bed with you, west side room.
>
> New writing plus access is really important tradition. Like one storm song. Something needed. And that's it. I want to say that much.

The End.

Navigating the Portal: A Deaf Artist's Journey Through the Pandemic

Chris Dodd

Award-winning artistic director and playwright Chris Dodd is the founder and artistic director of SOUND OFF, Canada's national theatre festival dedicated to Deaf performing arts. Chris was nominated for a Governor General's Innovation Award, and has toured his solo show *Deafy* across Canada. In his essay and spoken word poem, Chris explores his experience as a Deaf artistic director during a pandemic, and what lockdown opened up.

To say that the pandemic was an interesting experience for me as a Deaf artist is a bit of an understatement.

A mere seven months after the start of Covid, I decided to commit to becoming a full-time artist and quit my job at the University of Alberta. This shift happened in October of 2020, at which point I had already been working at the university for twenty years.

However, this was no snap decision. I had already been planning for several years to make my exit from my day job. My two daughters were growing up and my family life became less reactive and more of a stable hum. My wife and I had been carefully managing my finances in preparation for this shift, which included selling our bungalow in a leafy-green neighbourhood to move to a cheaper condo on Edmonton's south side.

My job at the university was as an adaptive technologist for the office of support services for students with disabilities. While almost entirely unrelated to my drama degree, it still allowed me the pleasure of supporting my students and seeing them prosper with the proper technology tools and support. At the same time, the Deaf theatre festival I had founded in 2017, SOUND OFF, had wrapped up its fifth year safely in January, when Covid seemed to be a world away.

My artistic practice has slowly been growing over the years, and helming SOUND OFF compounded that. Prior to 2015, I had very little opportunity or engagement as an artist, and it was difficult for me to find a place for myself as a Deaf artist. There were so few opportunities available to me that, for a point over a period of years, I gave up entirely on my dream of being a performing artist. I did not see theatre, I did not read about it, nor did I connect with my friends within the mainstream community.

However, thanks to an increased focus on diversity and inclusion, in many different areas, including our mainstream theatre community, theatres have been waking up to the historical wrongs and the systemic exclusion faced by artists like myself and others on the margins. Slowly the opportunities built momentum, and I found myself increasingly engaged.

These opportunities were not only as an actor, but also for myself as a dramaturge, playwright, director, and consultant. As the demand for my skills and repertoire grew, I was faced with the difficult task of trying to juggle full-time work with an artistic career that was rapidly ramping up.

So, once the opportunity was right, even though it was at the start of a global pandemic, I plunged myself headfirst into a career of being a full-time artist.

Of course, at the time there were many uncertainties. I was concerned for myself, as well as for others within the Deaf and Disability Arts community, that the pandemic would stall our growth and set back the progress our communities had been making up until this point. Would our battles for inclusion, as both audience members as well as artists both onstage and behind it, be pushed aside as unimportant in comparison to other struggles during this transition?

However, the pandemic was full of surprises, as well as engagement. Even though I was stuck at home, at my computer, in the basement office in the corner of one room with only a small window that remained my connection to the outside world, I was still engaged more than I had ever been before.

Because everything moved online, the programming of several dozen theatre organizations across the country suddenly became available to me, because they had all scrambled to shift their programming to virtual spaces, which, in turn, opened them up for participants from outside their communities. Suddenly I was spoiled for choice. While not all events were accessible, a good number of organizations started adding accessibility to their events with ASL interpretation, most likely due to budget surpluses, which meant they could suddenly afford accessibility, despite not having planned it within their yearly budgets.

Of course, ASL is a three-dimensional language, and it flourishes for in-person interactions rather than two-dimensional screens. Despite that, Deaf artists have always been ahead of the curve for integration of technology when it means we can better communicate and better disseminate our ideas and stories. In the absence of being able to gather and interact in person, being able to connect online was a godsend.

The soon-to-be-favoured teleconferencing platform, Zoom, started off with abysmal accessibility but slowly evolved, through feedback and complaints, into something more workable. The most important revision was the inclusion of auto-generated captions, which were introduced toward the end of 2021. While not perfect and certainly no replacement for true access with an ASL interpreter, these captions still provided minimal accessibility for each and every single online event.

Suddenly I was confronted with the privilege enjoyed by hearing and able-bodied artists and, through the evolution of technology, finally found parity with my peers.

Of course, captioning isn't just for those who are Deaf – it also benefits those who are hard of hearing (especially our older generation), those who have English as a second language or those who have challenges such as auditory processing disorders or autism.

Beyond my own community, online meetings can also be a lifeline for those who can't easily attend in-person gatherings. This could include those who are immunocompromised, people with social anxiety, and those with mobility issues, who worry whether the venue they are going to is accessible, and about the need to book accessible transportation a week in advance. These examples are just a small sampling of those who have benefited from this new paradigm.

Hence the irony and paradox that it took a pandemic to bring about the changes in the status quo and to shake ourselves out of our normalcy and allow us to look at things through a different lens.

At the same time, following the safety of our January 2020 festival prior to Covid, 2021 marked a challenging time; we had realized late in 2020 that conditions would not improve and that government restrictions related to live performance would continue. So we made the decision to transition the SOUND OFF festival to being entirely online. This meant throwing out the playbook we had carefully created for the previous five years and re-examining how we could continue to boost, support, and highlight our Deaf artists during this challenging time.

This involved curating filmed digital performances in place of our live shows. Our workshops, which normally took place in the breakout rooms of our Arts Barns venue, shifted to being online over Zoom. As well, our annual improv collaboration with Rapid Fire Theatre, involving an evening of both hearing and Deaf artists onstage, shifted to a new format online under the new name of *Maestro*.

The final results spoke for themselves. We were able to offer five digital performances on demand, along with one performance that was featured live, with the world-renowned immersive company Outside the March. Also included were six online workshops, two staged readings by Deaf playwrights, and two salon panel discussions. At the end of our festival, we featured a final wrap-up event over Zoom, *Deaf Party*, which included performances by thirteen Deaf artists from across Canada.

The interesting thing about being pushed to offer the festival as a fully online event was that it allowed us to reach out to our audience outside Edmonton for the first time. We had already billed ourselves as being a national festival from the start, and that still remained true, because we engaged with and brought in Deaf talent from across the country, from provinces including Alberta, Saskatchewan, Manitoba, and Ontario. But our outreach was still limited to in-person events in Edmonton, and the pandemic showed us the importance of being able to reach out and help celebrate the talents of our artists outside of our regional area.

For our next festival, in 2022, we made the important transition to being fully hybrid. We returned to in-person events at our venue at the Arts Barns while at the same time providing a robust offering of online workshops, panels, digital performances on demand, and live-streamed performances. We also included one live show in our lineup for that year, *Mundane Mysteries: SOUND OFF Edition*, the continuation of our collaboration with Outside the March. This new edition was an adaptation of the online ASL edition we offered the year before that featured two Deaf artists as detectives who probed to solve a specific mundane mystery posed by their guest for that performance. The most important thing was that, thanks to the Edmonton Fringe, we were able to simultaneously stream the show live online to audiences across Canada and beyond.

For the past few years, we have been proud to continue with our hybrid format and ensure that we connect audiences from coast to coast, even as our mainstream peers have pulled back, citing collective digital fatigue.

Beyond just outreach, when digital events are done right, with the proper access supports, it speaks volumes about your organization's mindset for social justice and your connection to the communities you serve.

Of course, engagement, like access, is a matter of budgeting. And budgeting reflects your values.

Accessibility should never be an afterthought. I have been advocating for years that arts organizations should set aside funding for accessibility in their annual budgets so that these costs are anticipated and accounted for, as opposed to being tacked on according to whims or budget surpluses. If more organizations across Canada planned their accessibility from the start, especially with multi-year budgets, this would have a significant impact on equity and normalize access as part of the theatre experience as much as pre-show cocktails at the theatre bar.

Furthermore, beyond just audience accessibility, we need a renewed budgetary focus supporting our Deaf and Disabled artists, ensuring that they have the resources they need in order to thrive in artistic environments and create authentic representation onstage. This also extends to those who are Deaf or Disabled who work behind the scenes, including designers, technical and administrative crew, as well as those who have authority in the decision-making process, such as board directors, general managers, and artistic directors.

Of course, this also means supporting our Deaf playwrights and directors too, to ensure that their stories, vision, and lived experiences are told in balance to the chorus of able-bodied creators.

All of this can be supported through improved access to training opportunities and peer mentorship opportunities, whether that means peers who share our struggles or peers within the mainstream who can help us move forward.

If there was just one thing we needed to leave behind at the start of the pandemic, it was the idea that we create art only for our own insular communities. Rather, this global pandemic helped connect us across this country in our shared struggles and loss, to find a common ground for a re-examining of what we have and what we hold dear, and the path forward.

Despite our gains, Deaf and Disabled artists are still undervalued, underengaged, underemployed, underrepresented on our stages. We need to claw back the digital momentum that was created under dire circumstances and reapply it as a tool for Disability Justice.

When used with proper accessibility, digital tools reach beyond one region or group and create far-reaching opportunities for Deaf and Disabled artists.

In closing, I want to share a spoken word poem that I created early in the pandemic. It was commissioned by Edmonton's Catalyst Theatre in response to the call to action by the National Arts Centre's Transformations Project, which sought to help artists articulate their perceptions of the new reality they found themselves in through the creation of new digital work.

Regrowth

Chris Dodd

SHOT 1

Intro: Fire

Music.

Fade to Chris, torso shot, doing the sign for 'fire.' Once Chris is fully in focus, he will sign 'spread.' These two words will not be captioned in the final video.

SHOT 2

Loss

CHRIS: *(signing, without speech)* Back when this all started, I thought to myself: 'What a loss.'

But not just me. Friends, family, neighbours, strangers

Everyone

Your opportunities
My opportunities

Gone
Vanished
Wiped out
Burnt

Music.

SHOT 3

Ashes

All that was left was ashes

Ashes of

What we knew
What we believed
What we dreamed
And what we hoped

Music.

SHOT 4

The Things We Lost

What we lost in this fire
We're not getting back
Or if we do, not exactly the same
Like a thing given to us anew

A gift from a stranger
With the best of intentions
A similar thing, but odd
Ill-fitting and awkward
Unaccustomed
And
Mystifying

Examining it
We try to make sense
But in the end find none

Music.

SHOT 5

The Paradox of Loss

But what did I really miss?

Many wondrous things

But I asked myself
Did I also miss the bad?

The talking mouths
Exclusion
Ignorance
Audism
The bias

Maybe these things were not really lost
But stealthily hidden
Scattered among the ashes
Waiting to be stirred again by my footsteps

Music.

SHOT 6

Balance

Nothing new can exist
Without the destruction of the old

As we go forward
There can only be renewal

A reexamining

Of

What we had and
What we hold
And what values we still cling to

With this regrowth

Comes the balance of nature
Rushing in
To fill a void

Music.

Regrowth

When you sign 'new,' it means 'to grow.'

Like life springing from your palms.

Start by imagining a tiny seed
Within the palm of your hand

Add to it

Your uttermost care
And love

Investing it with all your deepest hopes and dreams

Then watch carefully while it transforms

Music. Chris signs an ASL *segment demonstrating a seed growing into a radiant flower.*

SHOT 7

Change

We are ready for change

Ready for new stories
For new beginnings
New perspectives
Ready with courage

To accept the old ways are gone

Ready to build again
But this time better

Leaving behind

The ingrained defaults
The systemic standard
The so-called normal

Music.

SHOT 8

Evolution

It is a revolution disguised
As an evolution

A transformation

Of kindness
Of justice
Inclusion
Reconnection

And boldness

Of us looking ahead
And seeing
The endless possibilities
Stretched out before us
And being brave enough to embrace them

The cure is here. It is us.

Chris takes out a mask and puts it on. The lights around him fade out to black.

A Dramaturgy of the Senses

In Conversation with Audrey-Anne Bouchard

META award–winning theatre director and lighting designer Audrey-Anne Bouchard creates multisensorial, immersive performances for spectators living with or without sight. Based in Montreal, Audrey searches for new performance vocabularies, inspired by her embodied experience of vision loss. In conversation with Alex Bulmer, and in a script excerpt from her play *Camille*, Audrey explores how the language of lighting impacts her theatre making and what artistic opportunities are opened when imagining blind audiences.

Alex Bulmer: How would you like to introduce yourself and your work?

Audrey-Anne Bouchard: My name is Audrey-Anne Bouchard and I am a Montreal-based artist working in the performing arts. I was trained in design for the theatre and I have been working for fifteen years as a lighting designer in Montreal and internationally. I live with a visual impairment due to Stargardt disease, a degenerative condition that affects my central vision. Therefore, I only see with my peripheral vision.

In the context of my practice as a lighting designer, I came to the realization that the performing arts offer an experience that is primarily visual. I asked myself, 'How do people living with no vision at all experience a dance or a theatre performance?' Some of my collaborators and co-workers were also asking me, 'Do you think your visual impairment has an impact on the way you work with light?' These questions inspired me to think about my art in a different way.

In 2016, I initiated a research project called *Au-delà du visuel (Beyond the Visual)* with a team of interdisciplinary artists, including dancers and choreographers Laurie-Anne Langis and Marijoe Foucher, actor and writer Marc-André Lapointe, and sound and set designers Joseph Browne and Laurence Gagnon Lefebvre. Collectively, we explored the following research question: How can we create and communicate dance and theatre beyond the visual relationship that prevails amongst performers and spectators? Together, we developed a new immersive and multi-sensory art form that involves all the audience's senses except sight and is designed for an audience living with low vision. Through that research, we created our first piece, titled *Camille*, that was presented at the MAI (Montreal, arts interculturels) in 2019. I directed the piece and wrote its script with my collaborator Marc-André Lapointe. Since *Camille*, I have become more active as a director and a writer.

AB: How much does light continue to be a part of how you imagine theatre?

AAB: I do think that the language of stage lighting, my first medium, informs the way I create now. One function of light onstage is that it allows you to direct the gaze of the audience, bring their focus to different subjects and dimensions. It works a little like a camera in cinema. You can create a wide picture onstage and then zoom in on something more precisely. When I create scenes as a director, even if I am creating them with my eyes closed for an audience who is either Blind or wearing blindfolds over their eyes, I am interested in bringing their focus on different details. This allows me to transport the audience from one dimension to another. For example, a scene in *Camille* takes the audience into a restaurant. We created a loud restaurant environment around the audience, who is witnessing the characters having a dinner party at the next table. At some point, we leave the restaurant and dive into one of the character's minds, where he is having an internal monologue. In a visual piece, I would have changed the atmosphere with lights at that moment to illustrate the shift. Instead, my team and I use other languages, like sound, smells, storytelling, and physical interactions with the audience to travel from a restaurant into someone's mind.

AB: How do you draw the ears to pay attention to a particular moment? Listening is such a 360-degree experience, unlike seeing. How do you draw the ears into a particular focus?

AAB: It's a very good question. I believe that the experience of listening is different for someone who lives with blindness than for someone who is sighted and just experiencing wearing shades over their eyes for the first time in this context. We have realized that the pre-show introduction to our pieces is key in the experience we propose. It is essential to give the audience time to put on the eye shade and land, just sit and become aware of their other modes of perception. We begin the listening experience by playing the credits of the show in an audio format. This allows everyone to focus on the act of listening. Then I give information on how the experience is going to unfold and ask people if they have any questions. We spend approximately fifteen minutes just interacting together with speech and sound. The audience is then guided into the performance space, where we use different strategies to communicate with each spectator and keep their attention. Through the experience, we do not always want the focus to be the same for everyone. For example, at times we are performing different sounds in the space with our voices and with props, which creates quite an abstract ambient environment. Not everyone catches the same information, and each experience is unique. Some people will be attracted by the music and others will hold on to the text and the story. If there is a sound that is really important, we will make sure it stands out, and maybe we'll combine another sensorial stimulation with it. For example, in *Camille*, we supported a sound that brought the audience in a different location in the story by rotating their chairs 360 degrees simultaneously. In addition, text becomes part of the sound score and is important in our pieces because it guides the audience through the experience. It gives meaning to the sounds they hear, the atmospheres we create. All the languages participate in telling the story. In that mindset, we explore the potential of set, costumes, movements, and text to generate sounds and to keep the audience in that listening mode. People who are Blind or live with low vision read their environment through sounds in their daily life. They are not only used to listening but they can also process different information generated by many different sounds at the same time. For them, it is usually quite easier to follow the story with all its details and its many layers.

AB: It's really interesting. If I understand – and I was at the show, so I think I do – there is like a warm-up for the ears before you enter the actual space where the story will unfold.

AAB: Absolutely. I think there is a warm-up for the ears, and the piece was also designed to include an overall sensorial warm-up. With my collaborators, we had the desire to use different sensory stimulations throughout the experience. But we realized through the process that we have to introduce sensory stimulations one at a time. When touch is involved, that takes precedence over all the other senses. If a character is telling a story and you feel a hand on your shoulder, suddenly you are not listening to the story anymore and all your attention goes to the feeling of that hand on your shoulder – its pressure, its warmth, and what it makes you feel to be touched. We developed a dramaturgy of the senses as we built the show. At the top of the piece, when the main character first introduces himself and gives the premise of the story, we focus only on his monologue in order for the audience to capture what the piece is about. And then we slowly introduce different sensory stimulations and layer them so they interact together as the experience unfolds. At some point during the show, the audience becomes open to processing other sensory information as they get further into the story.

AB: Do audiences struggle managing the sensory interaction even though you're layering it? How have the audiences responded?

AAB: The experience is different and unique for every audience member. Once again, people who live with low vision are already trained to read their environment through sound and to be guided by other people in space. People who are sighted were surprised by how they reacted to other sensory stimulations. After the experience, some mentioned that they were surprised how they were attracted by smell or taste. Touch is definitely the most complex sense to work with and the most fascinating for the same reason! Not everyone is comfortable with touch, and we are putting a lot of work into integrating physical interactions in our pieces with care and respecting every spectator's comfort zone. I work with two brilliant choreographers, Laurie-Anne Langis and Marijoe Foucher, who are also massage therapists. They are trained to read the person they are interacting with through their body language. They have trained the entire team to be in constant listening and caring mode. Our pieces welcome only a small number of audience members per performance so that each person can be guided and touched with the proper care and time required. The story also accompanies the audience through their experience, guiding them through the sensorial journey we propose.

AB: Without a story, I would imagine it would become a sensory spectacle or a kind of sensory fun fair, which, if that was your intention, fair enough. But it seemed very important to me that there was an integration of character and story with these sensory experiences. Can you talk more about that?

AAB: Yes. In fact, the answer to this question emerged from our creative process. Inviting consultants living with low vision to experience our work in development is an essential part of our creative process. We call them our experts, for they bring a unique perpetual expertise to the work. Even though I live with a visual impairment myself, I feel it is important to gather a diversity of perspectives.

After a first year of research with my team of collaborators, in the context of which we explored the possibilities of creating and communicating dance and theatre beyond the visual, we presented our first explorations in the form of three tableaux to a selected group of experts. At that point, there was no story. Only the first tableau was exploring text. The main comment we received after the presentation was that the participants were not clear on why they were experiencing certain sensations and why we were inviting them in particular settings. For example, one of the tableaux was taking place in a forest. We were trying to create the atmosphere one might feel in the woods. The experts wondered why they were in a forest at that moment and what was expected of them in that poetic environment. My conclusion from the feedback we received was that for someone who can't see, there's nothing like being in a real forest. And trying to recreate that onstage became a bit artificial. I thought: 'Why don't we just do a multi-sensory performance in a forest?' In a theatre, you will never get all the depth and diversity of sounds and smells that you can get in an actual forest. And yes, what is the point? What if we were following a character in that environment or if the sounds of the leaves in the tree told a particular story? Another tableau was a dinner scene around a table. For my team, who was composed of partially sighted and sighted artists, wearing eye shades to smell and taste different foods and listen to the rhythm created by the sounds of dishes was very exciting. But for our experts, this was just daily life, another Tuesday night and nothing special.

It occurred to me then that telling a story would be a tool that could give meaning to all the sensations we were creating for the audience during the piece. For example, a performer is putting their head on my shoulder because they miss someone. In addition, if we want scenes like the dinner party to be extraordinary for people living with blindness, who are used to this setting, we can develop the characters and their relationships around the table and travel in the mind of one of them to have access to what they are feeling at that moment. The audience is then at the dinner table and in the character's internal space at the same time. Text became our best ally to create an experience that would be extraordinary for our audience members living with low vision and transport them in unrealistic situations that could communicate not just dialogues and locations but also emotional states.

Many times during our creative process, we had to remind ourselves that we were creating the piece for an audience living with low vision based on their perceptual reality and abilities. Our artistic choices would have been totally different if we had made them based on the comments of sighted audience members.

AB: And I suppose you can change settings simply by what people are saying, and then letting the audience understand where they are from the actual dialogue.

AAB: Yes. That is the beauty of also not having to deal with the visual codes onstage, allowing us to bring the audience from one location to the next in one sound cue.

AB: If someone who hadn't experienced your work was reading this thinking, 'Well, isn't that just radio drama?' how would you respond?

AAB: [Smiles] We are inspired by radio drama, of course, and it's a very interesting form of art as well. The difference in what we do is, first, in the essence of what theatre is – a communal space we share altogether and in which we are physically present. Our work is immersive, which means the action is happening all around you. You are sitting onstage, in the set of the piece, on a chair that was specifically designed for the experience and that offers tricks the regular chair cannot do. The soundscape is performed live and through a recorded score that is enveloping you. In addition, in the work we propose, the other senses are also coming into play. The cast performs physical interactions with the audience. For example, in one of the scenes in *Camille*, each spectator will be handed an umbrella the performer will help them place over their head. And rain will fall on it. Sound is certainly the main character of our piece, like in radio drama, but many other languages participate in telling the story.

AB: There was a scene in *Camille* set in a hair salon that represents everything we've been talking about so far. Can you tell us about it?

AAB: Yes, absolutely. It gives a good overall perspective on the multi-sensory and interdisciplinary nature of the art that we do. The scene begins with a dialogue between two men; one of them did not make an appointment, and at first the audience does not know where the scene is taking place. We hear the sound of a loud fan, scissors, hairdryers ... We slowly understand that the main character is coming to get a haircut. At that moment, the audience members are sitting in a hair salon. They are listening in on the conversation that is happening between the client and the hairstylist. They are in the present moment with the characters. And while he is getting his hair cut, the character experiences a memory that takes us into his mind, where we hear him talk with his childhood friend to discover that she will be leaving and that their friendship will end at the same time. Suddenly, the character and the audience hear the sound of scissors by their ears. This both takes them out of the memory and brings them back in the present moment. At the end of the scene, as the character leaves the hair salon, the audience receives an umbrella and feels the rain falling on it, evoking all the sadness of the character. This scene uses dialogues and flashbacks, and takes the audience into the character's mind. Through the piece, we invite the audience to take different perspectives. Sometimes they are witnessing the action, and at other times they find themselves in the position of the character.

AB: While in the show, one thing that struck me was how you removed the audience from the act of anticipation. There was no description of what was about to happen – nobody described that an umbrella was about to be put into my hands – it just suddenly was offered. Your play reflected my Blind experience of not being able to anticipate what's coming. I wondered how sighted people who aren't used to that, or those who may be supersensitive to sensory stimulation, respond and remain engaged.

AAB: Five years after the premiere of our first show, *Camille*, we are still challenged every time we introduce a new prop, sound, contact in the work. I can give an example of strategies we use: If we are producing sound with an object in the space, we start at a distance and come slowly closer to the audience, performing the sound in order for them to hear it come closer. Of course, we can't do this with physical contact. We do open the umbrella above the spectator's head before we give it to them, but it still remains surprising. That is part of the magic of the experience as well.

I think it is important to inform the audience that we are inviting them into a caring space. Our goal is not to provoke or to scare. We are expressing a range of emotions and atmospheres, therefore we are not always in a 'feel good' experience, but overall we want people to feel at ease and allow themselves to let go and just be with us in the present moment. Through our research, the team came up with one rule, which is that 'the spectator can do no wrong.' Let me go back to the example of the umbrella in the hair salon scene. Sometimes audience members do not take it in their hands; if the spectator doesn't grab the umbrella, the performer holds it for them above their head. We always have plans A, B, C, and we adapt the experience constantly to make sure audience members don't feel they are not doing what was expected of them, because that would take them out of the experience right away. There is, in fact, no right or wrong – just different ways to go through the piece and respond to proposed interactions.

It is more challenging for people who are sighted to cope with the fact that they suddenly can't see things coming and anticipate how they are going to feel or sound or smell. They already have to deal with the loss of their vision from the very beginning of the experience. People who are Blind are one step ahead. They will most likely grab the objects we present to them because that is how they experience interactions in daily life – with no anticipation, as you mentioned. In our pre-show introduction, I inform the audience that objects will be presented to them and there will be interactions. I also tell them they are free to interact as they wish, follow their instincts, and respect their comfort zone. In the moment, I think, people can't predict how they will react, and that's why we adapt. The same person could also react differently from one day to the next, depending on their mood of the day.

chose to tell a story about the loss of a friendship, about the one who stays behind, the character who lost his friend who brought him a sense of security in his life. Through the show, he is trying to create ties with new people, but it's hard, because it's new. And it's not the dynamic he's used to. The story is a metaphor for what we ask the spectator to go through in this piece: You lose your bearings, and now you have to learn to trust new people who are interacting with you in different ways. And you have to learn to trust that it's going to be okay, and to let go. To answer your question, our interactions with our audience are the premise for the story – we use those interactions to communicate how hard it is for the character to trust others and make contact with new people and to go through different experiences.

AB: Wow ... you could have just described what it's like to lose your sight. [Laughter] I think you just did. It's so much about trust and loss. And adapting and realigning with yourself and with others.

AAB: It was a consensus in the whole team that we didn't want to tell a story about someone losing their sight. Why focus on that specifically in the story when the form is already about that? But, of course, because we created it in dialogue with the community of people living with low vision and, with our eyes closed, I think it still informed a lot the artistic choices that we made, and the story that emerged from all of that. Loss is a very universal theme. I think people who have experienced loss in any way can relate to the story.

AB: Absolutely. Loss is experienced in many different ways, as is trust, as is the need for others and connection.

I do want to ask you a personal question about your relationship with theatre. Why is theatre important to you? And why is theatre important in terms of telling stories?

AB: That's fantastic. You've said so many interesting things and I do want to ask as we wrap up: Is there anything else you would like to say?

AAB: I would like to mention how wonderful it is to have this conversation about my work with a professional artist who is also living with low vision – it's a first for me. And it's really mind-blowing to realize how you experience and understand my artistic intentions. Thank you for asking me to be part of the great project that is this publication! I hope it encourages others to take inspiration from their different abilities to create new art forms and experiences that will speak to all.

Excerpt from *Camille: The Story*
Audrey-Anne Bouchard

Camille: The Story is an immersive performance specially designed to engage all of the spectator's senses – except sight – and is therefore entirely accessible to audience members who are Blind and to all audiences (ages twelve and over). People who are sighted and partially sighted must wear a blindfold from the beginning to the end of the performance.

Audience members are invited to enter the performance space and to sit at the centre of the set where the story unfolds. The small capacity of six audience members per performance promises an intimate, unique, and multi-sensory experience.

The indented italicized text describes the sounds and movements performed by the ensemble during the scene.

SCENE II

Hair Salon | November 15, 4:30 p.m.

> *Pierre stops his walk.*
> *Sound of a fan in the sound score.*
> *Pierre awkwardly shakes off his umbrella.*
> *Hair Stylist crosses the space to greet him.*

HAIR STYLIST: Bonjour! Hi!!

PIERRE: *(preoccupied with his umbrella)* Hello …

HAIR STYLIST: Do you have an appointment?

PIERRE: No, I don't. I didn't think … It's my first time here.

HAIR STYLIST: Were you hoping to see someone in particular?

PIERRE: I'm in a bit of a rush. Is anyone free now?

HAIR STYLIST: Yeah, me.

PIERRE: Oh, ah, okay, great. Thanks …

HAIR STYLIST: Just follow me.

Both men cross the space. Sound of a hairdryer.

HAIR STYLIST: *(speaking loud over the hairdryer)* Have a seat right here. What did you have in mind?

PIERRE: Huh?

HAIR STYLIST: *(louder)* What do you usually do with your hair?

PIERRE: *(loudly)* Usually … my friend cuts it for me.

HAIR STYLIST: Your friend's a hair stylist?

PIERRE: No.

HAIR STYLIST: Right. Okay. *(pause)* I guess they weren't available to cut your hair this time … ?

PIERRE: No.

The hairdryer switches to its highest intensity.

Beat.

HAIR STYLIST: *(louder)* Well … do they usually cut it short?

PIERRE: *(louder)* They've moved away.

The hairdryer is turned off in the middle of the sentence, leaving the last words resonating in the room that has turned to silence.

HAIR STYLIST: Right. *(pause)* So … would you like to try something new? For a change?

Excerpt from *Camille*

PIERRE: Maybe. Yeah. Why not?

Synchronized sounds of Velcro and of the movements of hair salon capes at different positions in space.

Hair Stylist starts a razor.

HAIR STYLIST: Ready?

PIERRE: I don't know.

Hair Stylist turns off the razor.

Beat.

HAIR STYLIST: Maybe you'd rather come back another day?

PIERRE: The thing is, I have this dinner party and I wanted to ... I just didn't want to look like a guy who's been stuck in his apartment for three months ...

HAIR STYLIST: Three months!

PIERRE: I mean, not literally ...

HAIR STYLIST: Your hair literally speaks for itself ...

Beat.

PIERRE: Thanks ... ?!

HAIR STYLIST: Listen, why don't we go slow. How about a trim? We could just freshen up the cut you already have. Your friend did a good job. It's got a nice shape.

Thermal water mist is heard in space and felt on the hands and arms of audience members.

Memory music brings the audience into Pierre's mind. The following sounds and voices are in the sound score.

PIERRE: Can I come in? *(silence)* Camille?

CAMILLE: I'd rather you didn't say anything, Pierre.

PIERRE: Why won't you come out of the bathroom?

CAMILLE: Stop talking, please …

PIERRE: Let me in! Camille, c'mon, open up!

CAMILLE: Talking won't help. Please, don't talk. *(pause)* Pierre, are you still there? *(panicking)* Say something, Pierre!

PIERRE: *(softly)* I'm here.

CAMILLE: Okay. Now, no talking. I just can't … I just can't be there for you right now, okay? It's not that I don't want to, it's just … I don't think you can help me … Not … not this time. Could you just say 'okay' so I know you heard me?

PIERRE: Okay.

CAMILLE: Pierre, I'm going away. I need to figure things out and I need to do it alone.

I know you won't agree. I know it. But just say 'okay' so I know you heard me.

Long pause.

PIERRE: Okay.

PIERRE returns to the present. The voices are live.

HAIR STYLIST: Okay!

Two clear scissor cuts are heard near the ears of each audience member.

PIERRE: *(alarmed)* Hey! Whoa.

HAIR STYLIST: You said 'okay.'

PIERRE: I didn't mean okay-okay!

> *Various and numerous sounds of scissors in space and around each audience member.*

HAIR STYLIST: Oh, sorry, I misunderstood … Not a problem, it's totally fixable.

PIERRE: I don't think this is going to work. *(He takes off his cape and throws it on the floor.)* My fault, this just wasn't a very good idea. I have to get going anyway, I have that dinner party, and now I'm late …

HAIR STYLIST: Wait. Don't you want me to … even it out?

> *Hairdryers and razors are turned on and manipulated in space at different levels and various speeds, creating a chaotic orchestra.*

PIERRE *exits. Rhythmic music fills the room.*

The razors come very close around each audience member. The warm blow of a hairdryer is felt around each audience member's head while another hairdryer swipes their feet.

All razors and hairdryers turn off in synchronicity.
  Umbrellas open in synchronicity.
  Music fades away.

Each audience member feels the gentle contact of an object on their forearm. They are invited to grab a handle. It is the handle of an open umbrella that is then placed above their head.
  Drops of rain start falling on the umbrella. The music of rain fills out the room as it is also heard in the sound score.
  The rain stops. The umbrella is gently removed from the hands of each audience member, leaving them listening to the inviting music of a piano.

Photo 1: The image is in black and white. At the centre, a male performer, seen from neck to waist, is facing right and standing at a round table. His hands rest on the table, on either side of a cup and saucer. In the background, two audience members sit on chairs facing us, one to the performer's left and one to his right. Both audience members are wearing eye shades. *(Featuring Marc-André Lapointe in the role of Pierre. Photo by David Wong.)*

Photo 2: The image is in black and white. In the foreground, at the centre of the image, a female performer holds in her left hand a diffuser emitting a scented cloud of vapour. Above the diffuser, the performer holds in her right hand a traditional hand fan, which she waves back and forth slowly, sending the pleasant scent toward an audience member sitting in a chair in the background. The head of the audience member is obscured by the fan. *(Featuring Laurie-Anne Langis and another performer. Photo by David Wong.)*

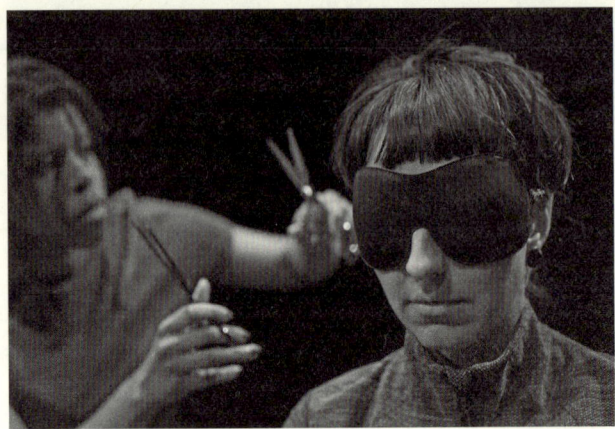

Photo 3: The image is in black and white. The right half of the image is a close-up of a female audience member from the shoulders up. She is wearing an eye shade. On the left, a female performer, slightly out of focus, is holding two pairs of scissors right by the woman's ear. The open scissors are about to close, producing a sharp sound. *(Featuring performer Alexandra Laferrière. Photo by David Wong.)*

Photo 4: The image is in black and white. In the foreground at the bottom left corner sits an audience member wearing an eye shade and holding an umbrella over her head. At the top right corner of the image, a performer holds in her right hand a colander, from which rice falls onto the umbrella to evoke the sound of rain. *(Photo by David Wong.)*

Black and Indigenous Disabled Magic, Creativity, and Practice: Defining Our Work on Our Own Terms

Dr. Syrus Marcus Ware in Conversation with Theodore Walker Robinson and Raven Davis

Vanier scholar and artist Syrus Marcus Ware has an extensive leadership history including co-founding Black Lives Matter Toronto and the Wildseed Centre for Art and Activism. He received the TD Diversity Award and the Steinert and Ferreiro Award for inspired contribution to the 2SLGBTQ+ community.

In discussion with artists Theodore Walker Robinson and Raven Davis, he considers white supremacy in the arts, emergence, and how Disabled artists set up their practices in ways that honour their bodies/minds. Included is an excerpt from Syrus's play *Antarctica*, first produced at the Toronto Biennial of Art.

Syrus Marcus Ware: Thank you so much for the chance to have this conversation today. Welcome, Raven Davis and Theo Walker Robinson! It's such an honour to get to be part of community with you and to be Disabled artists making work together in these times. Can you tell me a bit about your practice?

Theodore Walker Robinson: I am Theodore Walker Robinson. I use they/them pronouns. I am a low vision and hard of hearing and Mad artist. My practice right now currently focuses on weaving methodologies for Blind and low-vision folks using a myriad of different materials. I started my practice using the traditional fibres of yarns, but now I'm looking into sustainable materials like mechanical and electronic waste to create tapestry and African-inspired weavings.

I'm also a music producer and I have an interest in creating soundscapes and song projects inspired by African house music and electronic dance music. And that's part of my practice as it stands right now. It's always evolving, but right now those are my two disciplines – music and weaving practice.

SMW: Amazing.

Raven Davis: Thanks, Theo. I always love hearing about your work. Thanks for the intro, Sy. My name is Raven Davis. I use they/them pronouns. I'm a Two-Spirit queer, trans, and Disabled multidisciplinary artist, mediator, and educator. I'm also a parent to three incredible sons. My practice includes visual art, movement, performance, sound, and ritual. It's deeply embedded in research within colonial histories and lived experience.

SMW: It's really hard to encapsulate a lifetime of creative practice, especially when it's so interwoven with our lives. I think this weaving our art into our daily lives is actually something Disabled, Deaf, and Mad artists do. We integrate our creative practice into our everyday life.

RD: Truly. Having the cognitive capacity and resources it takes to be able to think about all of your practice, to be able to speak it and to summarize it in a few words, I've always found it really difficult. So I usually encourage people to come out and see it and experience it in different ways, as opposed to just reading a bio or reading about a piece I've worked on. Engaging with my work in different accessible and sensory access points, prioritizing human relationality and dialogue.

SMW: How would you say that disability intersects with your creative practice, if it does?

TWR: I've heard it said and I've said this a lot with the people I mentor who are Disabled artists: To be disabled is inherently creative. To make something accessible is inherently creative. By nature we are inherently creative beings, and everything we do is some kind of innovation on something, some kind of new iteration of something, or the creation of a brand-new world.

Every space we enter – we change it in some way. Through making people conscious of how to interact with us, that's a creation in and of itself. I find that my practice is not only just the artwork I do in my studio, but my practice extends to creating change no matter what room I walk into, because there's something new created. Whenever I encounter access needs in my own business, or through being a Disabled executive in the office, it is something so new that people are scrambling trying to create something brand new for me. I find the practice itself is inherently creative. To be Disabled is creative, and that's what identifies Disability Arts for me.

RD: Yeah, I totally agree with you, Theo. Just echoing that each moment, as Disabled artists, we adapt to spaces. We adapt to communication. We adapt to structural spaces. We adapt to sound spaces. And within that we are creating in each of those moments. I really appreciate what you shared there. Disability Arts definitely has given me permission to not be siloed into creating within one medium and method. In the mainstream world: You're a visual artist, that's all you do. You just do visual art. You're a sound artist, that's all you do. You just do sound art. And as an interdisciplinary artist, as a Disabled artist who uses different mediums, I feel disability has allowed me to say, 'No, Disability Arts, to me, it means I can use any material and in any way.' That fuels me to break down the 'fourth-wall' and encourages the viewer to have a multidimentional and relational experience. I can create anything from paint to sculptural to performance. The brilliance of Disability Arts creates portals of total, creative liberation.

SMW: I really have felt that working as a Mad artist, as a Disabled artist ... working in the ways that jive for my bodymind. So that means taking my time, having a bit of a different durational process than maybe traditional theatre artists who are not Disabled. You go into these theatre rooms and you're expected to do six weeks – six days on, one day off, five to six hours a day. That just doesn't work for me. So I've been trying to create rooms that look different and that feel different, that work with my bodymind. And then, as someone who does drawing and painting, again, working in ways that work for my body, I have something with my hand now – they think it's arthritis.

So working with my right hand is a challenge. I'm figuring out ways that work for me, and it's allowed me to be a creative practitioner in ways that could have longevity so that I could be doing this when I'm ninety. My grandmother is a ninety-seven-year-old artist and she's still making work, and she's doing it in a way that works with her brain. She has dementia now and she's doing it in a way that doesn't require her to have a consistent memory from day to day. She can still do her practice.

I'm curious about the intersections. One of the things that was so hard for me when I was first coming to disability studies as a discipline was how little they talked about racial justice. I wonder about Disability Arts and its connection to intersectionality. Often in Disability Arts in Northern Turtle Island, we don't always have a really good conversation about intersectionality woven in. As Black artists, as Indigenous artists, how have our experiences in our communities, in our cultures, come together in our understanding of Disability Arts?

TWR: White supremacy has its way of usurping all kinds of spaces, including justice spaces and disability spaces. I completely agree – even walking into Disability Justice spaces, I always find they are a lot of times white-led. They're the ones who are getting the funding to find people who represent people like me. Even within the non-profit organization that provides low-vision services to me, they told me once we're having a really hard time registering and enrolling Black low-vision and Blind people to receive the services they need.

There's the problem of white supremacy and then there's also the problem of racialized people also feeling there isn't enough representation of themselves. And so they don't seek out Disabled community because they have that feeling that there isn't anyone else out there like them. So I think it's kind of a double-edged-sword problem.

I mean, those who are the most resourced are going to be the ones who are the most visible at times. The ones who are able to organize and get the funds to become a non-profit organization, charitable organization, the ones who are able to work their way up to become ambassadors and be picked as the faces of whatever disability or access branding. And those are the ones who tend to be pushed toward the front, whereas racialized, Disabled folks, our presence is still very minimal up here. We're not sought out as much because of that domination of whiteness within Disabled spaces as well. That's what I'll say for now.

SMW: What you're saying is so interesting because, of course, Disability Justice grew out of BIPOC communities. Things do get consumed and taken up in the mainstream, and then domination and white supremacy feeds its way in. Raven, what are you thinking about this?

RD: Well, such a great conversation. I know just historically the trauma and the harm that were perpetuated against Indigenous and Afro-Indigenous people within the medical system and being forced into non-consensual medical and psychological testing, testing on our bodies. Which was further used as a reason for psychiatric detention, as a reason to forcefully remove children from homes, and for incarceration. They were/are taking children away from parents who maybe admitted that they were depressed or had anxiety. Even just the smallest 'fault' in child-raising or how we showed up in community could be used against us.

There was a time I had a very, very bad case of vertigo, which created some walking issues, some speaking issues, for me. I was nauseous all the time, and the three times I went into the hospital trying to get help, they were like, 'Are you sure you haven't been drinking? Are you sure? You might be here for some drugs. Are you sure you haven't had any alcohol?'

And it's just like how white supremacy has infiltrated these larger systems to create ableism within the communities.

A lot of people don't want to come out and admit that they're Disabled even though they have legacies, historical legacies of trauma, that have been transferred from one generation to the next. People have more acceptance over some disabilities than others because of stigmas. Madness, I find, is not accepted. I have to be a 'happy' activist and talk about violence that has been perpetuated against me or against our communities with a smile on my face. You can't be an angry racialized person. There is an expectation that BIPOC people should not show any emotions other than calmness and peace, despite the harms perpetuated against us. Respectability politics are forced onto BIPOC people, which reinforces how and if we are acceptable to the dominant society. Which in itself is ableist.

TWR: To your point, there is so much mistrust between racialized communities and the medical-industrial complex because of what Raven has mentioned. That history of the experimentation done on racialized bodies and the disabling of racialized bodies in colonial context. It has created a sense of shame around being within a racialized and Disabled body, and there is a culture of shame around disability within colonized communities, as colonized bodies. Within the Caribbean community, it's a very shameful thing to even talk about this Disabled cousin you have, because maybe it has this sort of colonial enslaved memory of becoming Disabled by a plantation owner, and now you're unable to work, and there's a shame that goes along with that.

Even in my family, when they've talked about my own disability growing up, there's a lot of shame and a lot of wanting to hide that around it. Whereas in other families, I've noticed, especially those more resourced families, there's a lot of championing of their abilities and what they can do. And look, my white Disabled child can do so much and can be visible in community, and they're given the resources they need to thrive. Whereas within a lot of racialized communities, there's a lot of shame pushed on the inability to participate in the economical context. Totally.

SMW: It always comes back to the Protestant work ethic and this idea of having to prove yourself as valuable by demonstrating how much you can work. And, of course, for a lot of Disabled, Deaf and Mad folks, that method is not going to work for us. Add in this layer of the arts – we already have an issue in the arts where there's still a whole bunch of firsts happening. First Black person to …, first Indigenous person to … do whatever. Because there have been so many ways that we've been underrecognized in those spaces. And I love this idea of underrecognized as opposed to marginalized or as a 'minority' because, of course, we've been here, we were here, we just weren't recognized as being here.

So in underrecognized communities in the arts, we often are having to fight so hard just to get to be in these artistic spaces and fight again to stay in them. So when we get to hear about the first Black woman to win an Emmy or an Oscar or whatever, which is recent, or the first Black artist to be at the Venice Biennale for a Western country or whatever, we're often hearing about these things without recognizing that this is all in spite of the arts. Not because of justice in the arts, but in spite of its lack of justice.

These Black artists and Indigenous artists are not succeeding because the arts have supported them. They're doing it in spite of the racism they're experiencing in the arts. They're still making incredible work and rising to this level of achievement.

I'm curious, of course, about the future. I love dreaming a little bit into the future. We know that there are issues with white supremacy in the arts. We know that there are issues of white supremacy in disability communities, and we know there's a lot of ableism generally in our social world that we need to fight against.

But also, we know we're building something new. We're building communities. We're fighting. We're uniting, we're coming together, and we're making beautiful spaces where BIPOC Disabled, Deaf, and Mad folks can thrive. We are. We're building it every day just through our community work and through our creative practice. What are you dreaming into for your Disabled artist's future? What are you hoping to see come and what are you dreaming will be happening in the next ten years?

RD: Basic income. Basic income! The freedom when social determinants are met: housing, food, health support, mental health support. Just the ability to create art and to contribute to our overall liberation through the arts, our collective liberation through the arts, without having to be pressured within capitalism. Without having to be 'productive,' or to have to make something that has to sell, to make something that has to be in gift shops. Instead I want to make art that creates conversation, connection, and belonging with each other. That's what I'm hoping for.

TWR: Yeah. I think that's something I'm still trying to formulate for myself, and what that means, just because my artistic career really didn't get started until the past couple of years. It really didn't start to really lift off the ground until recently. But I would love to see my work become recognized internationally. I'd love to be reintegrated in the international academic world again. It's been some time since I've been in the academic world, and this time when I do re-enter, it'll be me out and proud as a Disabled and queer and trans person.

I mean, before, when I was in the academic world, disability was something I really had to hide. The culture around it, especially in the ivory tower, was that I had to hide it and make it look like I could do particular kinds of work. I had to pretend I didn't have a disability of any kind. And I think the way I'm going to be approaching it when I'm back in school is that I'm here with this disability and I'm working with it and not against it.

I'm learning to be in a different relationship with my body when it comes to working in the academic-industrial complex and being gentle with my body in the way that it produces, and producing in a way that makes sense for it on its own timeline, instead of really forcing myself to get through stacks and stacks of articles to keep up with the pack. Instead I'm creating my own standard of production that makes sense for my goals and makes sense for where I see myself within my field of research.

SMW: For Disabled, Deaf, and Mad emerging artists or artists who are just getting started, do you have any advice? As Disabled artists who have been doing this for a while, Disabled and Mad artists, do you have any advice for artists who are just coming up, who are maybe trying to set up an artistic practice that works for their bodyminds?

TWR: I would definitely say don't compare yourself to non-Disabled artists in any way. I mean, you can enjoy their work, or appreciate their aesthetic or whatever part they create. You need to still understand how your own timelines work and how you produce, and really focus on knowing your own body and how your mind creates and works. If you have access to it. Even getting therapy to support you in figuring out the best way for you to create so that it doesn't make you feel as though you're a) exploiting your trauma, your Disabled trauma, and finding a way to create so that you receive joy from it, and b) not necessarily creating from a place of pain or trauma, only because what I do find a lot in the greater world of art consumption is that when they encounter a Disabled artist, they want to know about the trauma and the pain of it, and the clash between the able-bodied and the non-Disabled or the Disabled. They don't want us to be multi-dimensional beings with joy and full lives. Learn to really find your source of joy and create from that, because the world doesn't want to see Disabled joy. But we need it!

The mainstream art world really wants to prove its point that Disabled bodies aren't to be desired, and Disabled bodies are not useful in the economy. Instead, create in spite of that, and find that source of joy from what you can create.

RD: We could go on for hours! I love you both so much for this conversation.

I would definitely say, just gather support around you. Gather people who want to see you thrive, because it's not easy to always advocate for yourself ... to feel supported so that you can go in there and speak about your practice and feel proud of it and not allow others to dehumanize you because disability is also part of your identity.

They see value in our work because we're bringing a depth that not every artist brings to their practice, and we're bringing methodologies that not every artist understands, because Disability Arts is not taught or celebrated. It is, more often than not, looked at as an act of charity to present art by Disabled artists as opposed to what Disability Arts can teach and inspire in others. I'd say, keep going, gather the people who want to see you win in this world, and put aside competition, put aside comparing each other, comparing each other's practices, and just make work from the most authentic place possible.

SMW: Beautiful. Well, it's been such a pleasure to chat with you both today. Thank you for the work that you make and that you put out in this world. Thank you for the way you're living your life and showing us how to be in relation in a good way with each other and with land. And thanks for all that you offer to this world.

Excerpt from *Antarctica*
Dr. Syrus Marcus Ware

Characters

Sabian: A Black trans woman who is an activist in the United States before coming to Antarctica. She is anticolonial and abolitionist in leaning. She is a charismatic leader.

Marcus: A Disabled racialized person who does not believe in the company but comes along on his mission in order to have adventure and change in his life. He is a botanist and is interested in mushrooms and mycology in particular.

Jessica: A Black woman who believes that by fulfilling her mission she will be helping her family and fellow citizens. She is the least interested in Sabian's wild plans and she resists any deviation from the plan. She is a nervous person and spends her time counting her rations and worrying about the future.

Eugenio: An enigmatic stranger who the Antarcticians meet when they arrive in Mary Byrd Land. They are queer and racialized and possibly trans or non-binary. They are a scientist, and they have come to Antarctica to find peace and safety. They don't believe abolition is possible.

Marsha/Voice-Over: A narrator voices the second act, and we find out at the end that she has a special relationship to Jessica and Sabian. Could be played by actor playing Jessica.

ACT TWO, SCENE ONE: ICE FLOE ONE

Marcus, Sabian, and Jessica are on an ice floe in the middle of the stage. Sabian is sleeping. There are water projections on the rear wall. Marcus is sleeping too, at first. Jessica's vomiting wakes him. She is pregnant.

MARSHA/VOICE-OVER: Do you know how it started? How we got here? I know, I know, the company's Antarctica orientation videos … but did you ever hear the real story? The story of the time before everyone got here: when it was just the four of them, in the forest?

Jessica is sick to her stomach again, and it wakes Marcus.

MARCUS: Eww, Jess. Fuck! You good?

Jessica keeps vomiting. Marcus rubs her back. She shrugs him off.

JESSICA: I'm fine.

She sits up, wipes her face, and leans back.

JESSICA: Fuck, I'm not fine. I'm pregnant.

MARCUS: Jessica!

JESSICA: Shhh. Sabian doesn't know.

MARCUS: So, it's Sabian's …

JESSICA: I think so, yeah.

MARCUS: How far along are you?

JESSICA: Maybe three months? Maybe four? I've been trying to track it.

Overcome, she begins to vomit again.

SCENE TWO: ICE FLOE TWO

Marcus and Sabian are sitting up, talking. Jessica is asleep.

MARCUS: We've been swimming for days. Are we even on the right track?

SABIAN: The navigation says we are close: maybe two more days in the water.

MARCUS: I'm so ready to stop swimming. These rests are something but not enough. I feel so wiped out.

SABIAN: Yeah. Hey, Marcus …

MARCUS: Yes?

SABIAN: When we get there … I … It's just … what if people don't join us … what if we can't get …

She trails off. Sabian turns away.

SABIAN: Never mind.

MARCUS: *(puts his arm around her)* Hey, we're gonna make it there. Two more days.

SABIAN: But when we get there, then what? I spent so long convincing you to come, I guess I never thought you would, that we'd get this far …

MARCUS: Wow, Sabian, I never see you worried.

Sabian straightens up and speaks in a strong voice.

SABIAN: Marcus, I'm not worried … I'm just … wondering. What's next?

SCENE THREE: ON THE SHORE

A rear wall projection shows animation of the three swimming and landing on the shore. They land on the shore of a beach: there are exposed rocks and very little snow. There are plants growing, including moss and lichen on the rocks. The three pull themselves out of the water. They use their suction dryers to soak most of the water out of their suits, but they are still damp and cold.

Jessica, Marcus, and Sabian are on stage right, washed ashore. Stage left is dark.

JESSICA: There are plants here. Marcus, why are there plants here?

MARCUS: Moss, lichen, sphagnum ... How are these here? There haven't been spores planted yet: none of the colonies have started terraforming. And here in the vacant territory: there should be nothing but ... snow.

SABIAN: Well, this is great: if this land is already turning, we will be even further along when it comes to terraforming for our community ...

MARCUS: No, this doesn't make sense. I think we should be careful.

SABIAN: Let's go over the rocks there and see what's beyond them: we can lay low, just in case ...

The three crouch low and climb over the rocks into a valley.

A projection shows POV walking through the forest until coming upon a field.

Sabian and Jessica and Marcus arrive on the edge of the stage: looking from their vantage point in the forest onto a meadow with a multicoloured dome on stage left. There are plants and gardens surrounding the dome.

SABIAN: A forest?! Now this doesn't make sense! How is this here?

JESSICA: Look!

She points at a house in the centre of the forest. It is a large dome house with no windows and covered in bright textiles. They huddle close on the edge of the stage.

JESSICA: *(hisses in a whisper)* What do we do?

SABIAN: We knock. This land was supposed to be for our free community. We should find out who is living here and if they're a threat.

MARCUS: And what if they're company?

SABIAN: Company doesn't look like this. Think about it: everything about the company was white: our land, the people, our uniforms ... This is the most colour I've seen since we got here.

JESSICA: I think we should go back to the beach and set up shelter: it will be dark soon enough.

MARCUS: Unless they're friendly, and we can take shelter in that dome?

JESSICA: Fuck, you're so trusting! You really think the best of everyone?

She realizes that she is outnumbered.

JESSICA: Fine, let's go check it out: but let's be ready for anything.

They sneak toward the dome.

Marcus walks around the structure, trying to look inside. There are no windows. Jessica pulls him away from this circumnavigating and draws him back toward the door. Quickly, Sabian knocks on the door while Jessica and Marcus are distracted. Jessica lunges and grabs her hand.

JESSICA: What are you *doing*? Do you have a death wish?

SABIAN: I'm cold, I'm tired, and this looks like someone's home, not a company outpost. Somebody had to do it.

She holds up a metal pot full of mushrooms growing. She shows Marcus. There are similar plants in various containers around the door jamb.

JESSICA: Look at all this colour: I thought all I would ever see was white after so long in our territories. Who lives here?

Eugenio has arrived behind them without them noticing.

EUGENIO: I do.

The three turn around to see Eugenio holding a big stick and a small knife.

Who are you and why are you here?

Everyone is silent.

Your uniforms ... Are you company?

The three look between each other before Sabian moves to speak.

SABIAN: We aren't company. We are free people looking for space to land safely. We came to Mary Byrd Land to try to find safety –

Marcus interrupts Sabian.

MARCUS: No, wait, Sabian. *(turns to Eugenio)* You're somehow living in a multicoloured dome house in the middle of a 'forest' on a large sheet of ice in one of the most contested areas of land on earth and you're asking us who we are and how we got here? That's bold, man. Who the hell are you and how are you even here? How come there is a forest here in Antarctica?

EUGENIO: So ... you're not company?

ALL THREE: No.

Eugenio lowers their knife and stick. They rush past them toward their door.

EUGENIO: I didn't think I'd see another person again. It's ... been a while.

Eugenio goes around and turns off his alarms and alert systems.

MARCUS: Care to tell us who you are? I'm Marcus, this is Sabian, and Jess.

JESSICA: *(correcting him)* Jessica.

MARCUS: Jessica ... Your turn ...

EUGENIO: Eugenio. I'm a scientist. I'm here to live in peace: I had to get away from the race wars. You too?

SABIAN: Us? It's a bit more complicated. We're Antarcticians. We were born here ...

EUGENIO: *(in disbelief)* No shit? Man, I watched all the news of your journeys here. I can't believe you survived being plopped down here: cut off from everything ... pawns in the company game: to distract everyone from the depleting resources. *(Realizing company will be on lookout)* Oh, shit: the company. They must be looking for you. Do they know you are gone? You're gonna lead them right to here ...

SABIAN: Oh, we survived, and we broke free, and no: we didn't lead them here: we … we covered our tracks. Company won't know for months.

EUGENIO: Come in.

The two exchange glances before Sabian leads Jessica and her across the threshold into the space.

Fade to black.

Stage lights up, we see the dome has opened and we can see the inside. There is a cot, a table and chairs, and a small kitchen area. There are science books everywhere and several microscopes.

SCENE 4 : EUGENIO'S HOUSE

We see them drying off their hair and settled on the floor about to drink tea in Eugenio's dome.

MARCUS: You have a lot of books about plants. How did you end up here in the middle of a forest? How is there even a forest here, on this block of ice?

EUGENIO: I'm … a scientist. From … well, I'm not really from anywhere anymore. I'm just here. I came here ten years ago and planted this forest, with my accelerators.

MARCUS: Those must be some accelerators! I'm a scientist too: a botanist. Mycelium and mushrooms, the one thing I thought didn't exist on this continent – not yet. But the moss: the lichen on the rocks on the beach.

EUGENIO: You swam here? You must have a death wish. How far did you have to swim?

SABIAN: We were in the water for twelve days.

Eugenio gets up to roll a joint.

MARCUS: Wow: actual cannabis, not just rations.

He is excited. He offers to help break up the flower.

EUGENIO: *(mostly to Marcus)* The company began cracking down on scientists back home. We were sounding the alarm about climate change, about the viruses, about the need for change. It wasn't safe to stay where I was ... I came here to try to start something new. I brought seeds and spores ...

SABIAN: *(mostly to Jessica)* Way to steal our idea.

JESSICA: Sabian!!

Marcus glances over at Sabian and puts his hands up to try to get her to chill.

MARCUS: We are ... in a transition and we're hoping to make a life for ourselves too.

Sabian stands and walks to the table where Marcus and Eugenio are sitting and rolling.

SABIAN: Have you claimed this territory?

EUGENIO: I'm not a colonizer. I'm a scientist.

SABIAN: They're not mutually exclusive.

EUGENIO: I wanted a place that was safe for me to do my research. Safely. Without government involvement.

SABIAN: There is more than enough land in this territory for us to share it.

EUGENIO: This forest is my home, as much as we can own anything. I want to stay here. I've lived here peacefully for years. Away from the company and away from the race wars. I've been safe here. I can let you stay here until you are rested up, but I think it's best we all go our own ways. You're right: there's space in the edges of the territory. It's open valley; the ice is melting faster than they ever predicted.

Eugenio gets up, joint in mouth, and walks to the kettle.

EUGENIO: The isolation gets to you, though.

They pick up the kettle and bring it back to the table. They pour the water in a random assortment of vessels: they live alone and have had no need for multiple mugs.

Marcus takes his tea.

MARCUS: In our territories, we were so isolated. I can relate. When I was first sent here, everything was white, everything was silent … It was nice at first. One day making border checks, I met Sabian, and through her met Jessica. We found each other and have been together since.

Eugenio shakes his head in disbelief. He takes a drag and starts smoking. He lights Marcus's joint.

EUGENIO: Man! I can't believe you were born in Antarctica! I can't believe they sent you there! What a racket! I remember the news reports of your missions – talk about a fool's mission. No rations and limited technology and hope for the best? It was ridiculous.

MARCUS: A fool's mission! But … I had nothing else to do, so I agreed to come and did what I could to survive. Till I met Sabian and realized I was just helping pave the way for the rich colonists to come and take over once our … usefulness was expended.

SABIAN: Look, Eugenio: we're here to start something new. A free state. We would welcome the chance to stay connected as we build toward our free community.

EUGENIO: I never thought anyone would want to come here. I have been here since before they sent you on that mission. I patrol the borders, walk the shoreline. I laid low here in the free territory. After all these years, I thought no one would find me. This is my land. My territory.

SABIAN: Sounds colonial to me.

EUGENIO: Building a state, even a free one, on this territory sounds like colonizing to me too.

Sabian and Eugenio stare each other down. It is tense. Jessica stands up and tries to soothe the tension by touching Sabian and guides her back to sitting. Marcus fills the space with talking.

MARCUS: The tea's good. Thank you. Let's all take a deep breath, friends. Nice … Why don't you tell us more about how you got here? How'd you avoid detection?

EUGENIO: You learn a few things, being here. The company is nothing if not predictable.

SABIAN: Now, that's true. When I started patrolling back at the base, I noticed …

They continue talking, and we hear Marsha start to speak over them.

MARSHA/VOICE-OVER: They talked for hours that first day. Eventually they agreed to try to share the space, with the agreement that the Antarcticians would move south when the weather was warmer to set up their community. They would leave Eugenio to their privacy.

Underneath the voice-over, we see them building a second dome structure, cooking together, planting together, and time passes.

Breaking Barriers: My Journey from Saskatchewan to Shakespeare and Beyond

Dawn Jani Birley

Award-winning actor and cultural leader Dawn Jani Birley is the founder of 1s1 Deaf-led theatre, bringing Deaf-led stories to the stage. Working in both Scandinavia and Canada, Dawn won the Toronto Theatre Critics Award for best actress in her role as Horatio in *Prince Hamlet* in 2017, and is a recipient of the Canadian Cultural Society's Deaf Person of the Year award and the King Charles III Coronation Medal. In her essay below, Dawn contrasts her experience as a Deaf actor in Canada and Finland and details the extensive creative gains of Deaf-led theatre. Also included is an excerpt from *Prince Hamlet*, created with Toronto's Why Not Theatre.

When I was offered the role of Horatio in *Prince Hamlet*, I couldn't believe it. Opportunities like this rarely come my way. Most of my life has been about fighting for recognition, carving out spaces where none existed, and proving my worth in a world that often overlooks people like me. Born Deaf into a third-generation Deaf family in Saskatchewan, I grew up surrounded by a vibrant Deaf community. Everyone around me used American Sign Language (ASL), and communication was never a barrier – until I entered the hearing world.

Early Life and First Challenges

As a young child, I believed the world was made up of Deaf people. It wasn't until I started school that I realized how different I was perceived to be. I was thrust into an environment where everyone communicated using their mouths and ears, something I couldn't understand. My mother explained how hearing people used their voices, while we used our hands and eyes. Although I accepted this difference, the hearing world often turned it into a problem.

Throughout my childhood, I was told I couldn't do many things simply because I couldn't hear. Despite countless examples of Deaf individuals, including me, proving their capabilities, society still measured us by what we couldn't do rather than what we could. It wasn't until I studied Deaf culture and history at Gallaudet University that I fully understood the systemic roots of this prejudice, known as audism. Learning about the Milan Congress of 1880 – a pivotal event where sign language was banned in Deaf education – was a turning point for me. This historical injustice plunged the Deaf community into what felt like a 'Dark Age,' and its repercussions persist today.

Finding My Passion for Theatre

My mother played a critical role in nurturing my creativity. She would sign lullabies and stories, bringing characters to life in ways that mesmerized me. I loved dressing up, creating stories, and performing with my younger sister, but my dreams of joining the school drama club were crushed. When I pointed out that Marlee Matlin had won the Academy Award for Best Actress in 1987, I was dismissed with comments like 'That's an exception.' Instead, I was steered toward writing, drawing, and painting. While I excelled in these areas, my dreams of performing were fading away.

In 2000, everything changed when I saw my first sign language theatre production, *Karius og Baktus*, by Teater Manu in Oslo. I was stunned to see professional Deaf actors performing onstage and actually getting paid for it. Discovering that Deaf actors thrived in Norway, Sweden, and Finland gave me hope. Canada had never offered me such opportunities, so it was no surprise that I eventually found my way to Scandinavia, where I trained under prominent Deaf and hearing teachers. Fast-forward twenty-five years, I was cast in the leading role as Lysistrata in Teater Manu's production of *Lysistrata*.

Breaking Through Barriers in Education

While pursuing my master's degree in physical theatre, I faced yet another challenge. Despite being impressed by my application, the school hesitated to admit me because I was Deaf. After much persuasion and a successful audition, I was accepted, but my time there wasn't easy. My deafness was often treated as a problem, yet it became a powerful lens for my thesis. I researched the dynamics of working with hearing professionals, exploring how intersectionality shaped my creative process. My findings reaffirmed that intersectionality – acknowledging the unique and overlapping identities within a group – was far more effective than simple inclusion.

Despite graduating at the top of my class, I was told that creating shows for both Deaf and hearing audiences would be futile. Those words stung, but fate had other plans.

Horatio: Redefining Representation

When Ravi Jain, the director of *Prince Hamlet*, offered me the role of Horatio, my first question was 'Why me?' He explained that a conference he attended in the United States had challenged him to consider voices often overlooked and excluded, particularly in terms of accessibility. For me, it wasn't just about accessibility – it was about access to culture and language. My vision was simple: this production had to be for both signers and non-signers, a principle I had outlined in my thesis.

I reimagined Shakespeare through an intersectional lens, envisioning a bilingual production that seamlessly embraced both ASL and spoken English. Initially, inclusive thinking crept into the process, framing my deafness as a problem. For instance, I was asked, 'How will the hearing audience understand your signing?' My response was straightforward:

'How will the Deaf audience understand your talking?' This shift in perspective allowed us to craft a world where deafness was not an obstacle but an integral part of the narrative.

If Horatio was Deaf, it followed that others in the kingdom would logically know ASL – especially Hamlet, Horatio's closest friend. This approach not only enriched the story but also resonated deeply with audiences. Our cross-cultural, gender-bent cast further challenged traditional notions of who could tell this story, adding depth and nuance to the production.

The success of *Prince Hamlet* proved that embracing intersectionality can break down barriers. Many Deaf audience members had never set foot in a theatre before and were profoundly moved to see themselves authentically represented onstage. This journey was not just about reinterpreting Shakespeare – it was about showing what's possible when we build spaces that truly include everyone.

As a Deaf Actor, Double Work Is Inevitable

There is a recurring reality that sets Deaf actors apart from the rest of the acting world. Every Deaf person is born bilingual – not by choice, but by necessity. Language exists in different forms, and for us, sign language is a completely distinct linguistic system from spoken or written languages. To navigate the world, we must learn at least two languages.

However, when it comes to acting, many hearing people don't realize that the work is doubled for us. A hearing actor can simply speak the words as written, but for Deaf actors, it's not that simple. We must translate the script from written text into sign language – an entirely different structure, with its own grammar, rhythm, and expressive depth.

Here's why this process is far more complex for Deaf actors:

1. Translation Process

Deaf Actors: When given a script in a written language (e.g., English), must first translate it into their natural sign language (e.g., ASL). This isn't a direct, word-for-word conversion – sign languages have their own grammar, syntax,

and structure. Translation takes time and can take up a lot of rehearsal time.
Hearing Actors: Read the script and say the words as written, focusing on delivery rather than translation.

2. Conveying Meaning, Not Just Words
Deaf Actors: Must adapt dialogue to fit the visual and spatial nature of sign language, ensuring meaning, tone, and emotion are conveyed naturally. A literal translation often doesn't work, so they must rephrase, restructure, or even reinterpret lines for clarity and impact.
Hearing Actors: Can simply memorize and deliver the dialogue as written, using vocal tone to express nuance.

3. Rehearsal and Memorization Challenges
Deaf Actors: Need additional rehearsal time to internalize their signed translation so it flows naturally. They often work with sign language coaches or translators to refine their delivery.
Hearing Actors: Typically focus only on memorization, without needing to modify the script.

4. Coordination with Non-Signing Crew
Deaf Actors: Need an interpreter on set to communicate with directors, fellow actors, and crew, adding an extra step to rehearsals and adjustments.
Hearing Actors: Can instantly receive and respond to verbal direction without a third party.

5. Emotional and Physical Demands
Deaf Actors: Express emotions through facial expressions and body language as an integral part of their performance, requiring greater physical involvement than just vocal tone.
Hearing Actors: Can rely on vocal delivery for emotional expression, which is generally less physically demanding.

The double effort Deaf actors put in before they even start acting is significant. Recognizing this extra labour is essential for fair working conditions, better accessibility, and respectful collaboration in the industry.

Prince Hamlet (2017)

To be honest, if I didn't have years of experience and expertise – especially my talent in translation – my work in *Prince Hamlet* in 2017 would have been nearly impossible. My bilingual process was sometimes seen as a challenge, so I had to nudge Why Not Theatre to focus on the creative potential rather than seeing me as something to be 'solved.' As I mentioned earlier, with an audience of both signers and non-signers, the real question we needed to ask as a creative team was 'How will everyone understand both ASL and English?' It's not about accommodation – it's about integration. Theatre should reflect the world around us, not its limitations but its endless possibilities. However, what does accommodation really mean? Many hearing people assume they must accommodate Deaf people, but in reality it's often the opposite. From birth, we've had to accommodate the hearing world – adjusting, adapting, and navigating barriers in every situation.

Besides repeatedly reminding the team to focus on the process using the intersectional lens, I had to really work closely with Ravi on the text. In Why Not's version of *Prince Hamlet*, the show begins at the very end of the story, when Hamlet asks Horatio to tell the story of what really happened. This means that Horatio, as the main storyteller, has to translate *everything*, every line of each character in the story. To achieve this, staying true to Shakespeare, can be extremely challenging when converting his written word into visuals. Working on the translations, I had to deal with questions such as:

- Is this text direct or indirect?
- How do I preserve Shakespeare's metaphorical depth in translation?
- How do I achieve the poetry of Shakespeare in ASL?
- How do I make complex Shakespearean scenes visually accessible?

2. Authenticity: In a fully accessible production, Deaf actors or integrated ASL performers portray their roles as an inherent part of the performance, just like hearing actors do with spoken words. It's not about 'translation' of the dialogue through an interpreter. Deaf actors bring their own unique expression and storytelling style to the stage, just as hearing actors do, allowing for a more authentic representation of Deaf culture and experience.

3. Breaking down barriers: When interpreters are placed onstage, Deaf audience members often feel like the story is being filtered through a separate lens. The interpreter can sometimes unintentionally create a barrier, as Deaf audience members must watch the interpreter and the actors simultaneously, dividing their focus. In a fully accessible production, everyone sees the same performance, without needing to navigate a third-party translator, making it a more multi-faceted experience where the Deaf audience member isn't distracted from the action.

4. Multi-faceted design: A show that is fully accessible takes into account visual and performative elements in ways that are not typically considered when interpreting. It allows for a complete integration of visual cues, ASL, and lighting that enhance the experience for both Deaf and hearing audiences. For example, subtle nuances in ASL are often enhanced in an accessible production, using movement and space to express the full emotional depth of the scene.

5. Cultural sensitivity: Fully accessible theatre isn't just about adding a language; it's about embracing and respecting the cultural aspects of the Deaf community. While interpreters can convey the words, they cannot always fully capture the essence of Deaf culture and the nuances of ASL that are vital to the experience. By designing a performance that is accessible from the ground up, the show honours the culture in a way that interpreting alone cannot.

Ultimately, a fully accessible performance creates a shared experience, where all members of the audience, regardless of their hearing or signing ability, can connect with the story on the same level, without the need for intermediaries. It fosters a sense of belonging, allowing everyone to experience the same emotions, drama, and beauty of the performance.

Prince Hamlet Third Run (2022 – American Tour)

The third time we staged *Prince Hamlet* for the tour in the United States, in 2022, half of the cast was new. Unlike in the previous runs, the new cast did not have the ASL fluency and depth of understanding, and the production didn't uphold the bilingual process – something that made a huge difference. A hearing actor must learn how to work with a Deaf actor – it takes time, effort, and a willingness to overcome cultural barriers. We didn't have that time. Because of this, the bilingual nature of the show – which was critical to its success – wasn't as fully realized.

The entire show rested on my shoulders, as I had to start from scratch – learning each new actor's body language, their interpretation of lines, and their signing ability, all while building a new dynamic with a new Hamlet. I had to individually adapt to each of them, accommodate their strengths, and fill in the gaps as best as I could to recreate *Prince Hamlet* within a time crunch. But even then, it wasn't enough because it's crucial for non-signers and especially new cast members to receive Deaf cultural awareness training and ASL classes from the start, to prevent cultural misunderstandings that could negatively impact the production. These experiences reinforced the reality that Deaf actors carry an unseen labour – not just in translating text to sign, but in educating, adapting, and bridging gaps between languages and cultures. The real question is: When will the industry start seeing this not as a burden, but as an artistic advantage?

Why It Matters

For hearing actors, directors, and productions working alongside Deaf actors, cultural sensitivity and Deaf awareness training are essential – not just for inclusivity, but for authenticity, respect, and effective collaboration. Here's why:

1. Understanding Deaf Culture and Identity

Deaf culture is not just about hearing loss – it is a rich, complex identity with its own language, history, and values. Many hearing actors unknowingly bring misconceptions or stereotypes into their performances or interactions. Training helps them:
- recognize that deafness is not a disability but a cultural and linguistic identity;
- avoid offensive or outdated portrayals of Deaf characters;
- learn about Deaf norms, communication styles, and storytelling traditions.

2. Respecting and Working with Sign Language

Sign language is not a gesture-based version of English – it has its own syntax, structure, and grammar. Without training, hearing actors may:
- misuse or incorrectly sign phrases, leading to inaccurate or disrespectful performances;
- fail to match the emotional depth and nuances of sign language;
- overlook the visual and spatial aspects of ASL that are crucial for storytelling.

3. Creating an Accessible and Inclusive Workplace

Theatre is designed for hearing people by default. Without awareness training, hearing actors and crew may:
- unintentionally exclude Deaf actors from conversations and decision-making;

- rely on ineffective communication methods or adopt a patronizing attitude;
- fail to understand how to use interpreters properly;
- not realize how hearing actors can generally communicate easily and directly with everyone else and rely on verbal cues;
- not recognize how challenging it can be for a Deaf actor just to be present, especially when there are no other Deaf individuals involved, and lack the knowledge to provide proper support.

4. Strengthening Performance and Onstage Chemistry

For productions with both Deaf and hearing actors, seamless collaboration is key. Training helps hearing actors:

- understand the timing and the significant reliance on visual cues in bilingual performances;
- avoid talking over or missing signed cues, which disrupts the rhythm of the performance;
- develop a deeper connection with their Deaf co-stars, leading to stronger and more authentic storytelling.

5. Preventing Harm and Promoting Ethical Casting

Without proper training, hearing actors playing Deaf roles risk reinforcing harmful stereotypes.

- Deaf awareness courses ensure that hearing actors recognize why Deaf roles should be played by Deaf actors.
- Cultural perspective understands that Deaf actors bring lived experiences of Deaf culture, identity, and accessibility challenges to their performances, adding authenticity to Deaf characters.
- Hearing Actors typically lack direct experience with Deaf culture unless they've studied it or learned sign language, so if they are involved in a Deaf story, they should respectfully collaborate with Deaf creatives and consultants.
- Hearing Actors have historically been cast in Deaf roles, sometimes using sign language without deep cultural understanding, which can

lead to inauthentic portrayals.
- Deaf Actors often fight for authentic representation in media, advocating for Deaf characters to be played by actual Deaf performers.

Taking Deaf awareness and cultural sensitivity training is not about 'accommodating' Deaf actors – it's about ensuring equal collaboration and authentic storytelling, and breaking down systemic barriers. When hearing actors and colleagues invest the time to learn, they don't just improve their performances – they contribute to a more inclusive and respectful industry.

Inspired by the impact of *Prince Hamlet* in 2019, I wanted more. I approached Why Not Theatre, asking if we could pursue more work like that. They told me that if I wanted to see changes in our industry, I would need to take the lead – to push for the kind of transformation we achieved with their show. At first, I was scared. I knew I would face countless barriers – ones that could be time-consuming and discouraging, and potentially pull me away from my passion for artistic opportunities. However, I eventually realized that they were right, so with the support of Why Not Theatre, I founded 1S1 Theatre in 2019 – dedicated to breaking down those very barriers and creating a space where Deaf and hearing artists could collaborate as equals.

1S1 Theatre: Redefining Storytelling Beyond Words

Imagine a theatre where stories unfold not just through words, but through movement, expression, and the power of sign language. That's what 1S1 Theatre is all about: Deaf-led art to resist erasure. 1S1 Theatre is a Deaf-led company that reimagines storytelling, creating performances where Deaf and hearing audiences experience theatre as equals. Unlike traditional theatre, where spoken language dominates, 1S1 Theatre blends sign language and visual storytelling to craft powerful, immersive performances. Our productions challenge the idea that theatre is just about what you hear – it's about what you see, feel, and experience. Our mission is clear: to create Deaf-led productions, in fresh and innovative ways, to shake the status quo. For us, access is not an add-on, it is the aesthetic core. We invite hearing audiences into a Deaf worldview, not by diluting it, but by daring them to engage on new terms.

Our groundbreaking reimagining of *Macbeth (Lady M – Margaret)* and *Qalb – A Journey of the Ego*, inspired by Rumi's poetry and the realities of audism, received two Dora Award nominations and critical acclaim, showcasing the power of Deaf leadership in the arts.

Despite 1s1 Theatre making huge strides since its founding in 2019, it has been extremely challenging to secure venue, programming, and financial support. The reason we don't have Deaf millionaires, Deaf philanthropists, or Deaf executives in positions of power is rooted in centuries of systemic language deprivation and exclusion. Most Deaf people grow up without full access to language during the most critical developmental years of their lives. That deprivation limits educational opportunities, career advancement, and ultimately, financial independence. Many hearing people even do not know what language deprivation is, because there is no such thing in their world.

1s1 Theatre is crucial for Canada because it fills a major gap in the country's theatrical landscape by prioritizing Deaf-led, barrier-free storytelling. Here's why its work is so important:

1. **Bridging the Accessibility Gap:** Theatre in Canada remains largely inaccessible to Deaf audiences, with limited captioning, interpretation, or fully integrated sign language performances. 1s1 Theatre ensures that Deaf people don't have to fight for access – they can simply *belong*.

2. **Centring Deaf Culture and Language:** Unlike mainstream theatres that may 'add' accessibility features, 1s1 Theatre places sign language, Deaf culture, and visual storytelling at the heart of its productions. This creates theatre that is *made for* Deaf audiences rather than just *accommodating* them.

3. Deaf-Led Artistic Innovation: By having Deaf creatives in leadership roles, 1s1 Theatre challenges the dominant hearing-centric theatre model, proving that Deaf Gain – the unique contributions of Deaf people – enrich the arts.

4. Intersectional and Multifaceted Storytelling: The company's productions reflect diverse lived experiences, ensuring representation for marginalized communities beyond just Deaf identity. This pushes Canadian theatre toward true inclusivity.

5. Changing the Narrative on Disability and Art: 1s1 Theatre shifts the perspective from seeing deafness as a limitation to recognizing it as a creative and cultural asset, influencing how Canada approaches accessibility in the arts.

6. Paving the Way for Future Generations: By fostering a space where Deaf artists, actors, and creatives can thrive, 1s1 Theatre is building a legacy that ensures future generations of Deaf Canadians have a platform in the performing arts.

Canada prides itself on multiculturalism and inclusion, yet theatre remains largely inaccessible. 1s1 Theatre is leading the charge to change that, proving that accessibility should not be an afterthought – it should be the foundation of great theatre.

However, in truth, systemic barriers persist. In Canada, Deaf individuals often bear the cost of sign language interpreters, making it difficult to access opportunities. By contrast, Finland's government-funded interpreter services have been instrumental in my success. This stark difference highlights the need for policy changes in Canada to support Deaf artists.

Accessibility Inequities: The Stark Contrast in Deaf Accessibility Between Canada and Finland

As a Deaf person, I find that Finland stands out as a more inclusive and supportive country compared to Canada in several key ways:

Government Support for Accessibility

Finland takes accessibility seriously, treating it as a fundamental right rather than an afterthought. For example, the Finnish government fully funded the Canadian interpreters for all three *Prince Hamlet* productions and tours – something that would have been nearly impossible to secure in Canada.

The Finnish government provides comprehensive, fully funded interpreter services for Deaf individuals. This includes interpreters for education, employment, medical appointments, and cultural activities. This level of support ensures that Deaf individuals can access opportunities on an equal footing with their hearing peers, significantly reducing systemic barriers. This availability of interpreter services in Finland has enabled Deaf professionals, including artists, to thrive and pursue careers without being hindered by accessibility challenges. Finland's support was instrumental in facilitating my professional development and training in Scandinavia as well as my working in different productions all over the world.

In contrast, accessibility funding in Canada is often limited, inconsistent, and placed on the shoulders of individuals or organizations, making it difficult for Deaf artists to work on an equal footing with their hearing peers. Without institutional support, I likely wouldn't have been able to play Horatio at all – interpreting costs alone can easily exceed an entire production's budget, an expense no theatre company could realistically afford.

Too often, Deaf professionals are forced to cover these costs themselves, turning access into a privilege rather than a right. This financial barrier doesn't just limit participation, it actively excludes Deaf talent from opportunities that should be available to everyone. The lack of systemic support creates invisible barriers, making it significantly harder for Deaf artists to enter mainstream spaces, lead projects, or see their stories represented onstage and on screen.

Legal Recognition of Sign Language
In 2019, the Canadian government passed the Accessible Canada Act, which recognizes American Sign Language (ASL), Langue des signes québécoise (LSQ), and Indigenous Sign Languages as the primary languages of Deaf people in the country; however, this recognition is largely symbolic and does not grant them full legal status as official languages, like English and French. Access to services often depends on provincial policies rather than federal law. Some provinces, like Manitoba and Ontario, have taken steps to recognize ASL and LSQ in education and accessibility policies, but there is no nationwide legal framework guaranteeing full linguistic rights. Unlike Finland, where Finnish Sign Language is officially recognized and protected by law, Canada's recognition does not ensure systemic access to services, education, or employment in sign language.

Deaf Canadians still fight for interpreters in health care, education, and public services, often facing inconsistent or inadequate accessibility measures. Overall, how can Deaf Canadians advocate if the interpreting costs are not consistently covered by the government?

Equal Access to Education and Employment
Finland's education system provides strong bilingual education for Deaf students, ensuring they have full access to their native sign language while also learning written Finnish or Swedish. This creates a strong foundation for future opportunities. In Canada, Deaf education varies greatly by province, and many Deaf students are still forced into mainstream schools with inadequate sign language access, leading to lifelong disadvantages in literacy (as in language deprivation, which is serious in my Deaf community) and employment.

Cultural Inclusion
In Finland, Deaf culture and sign language are integrated into the broader cultural landscape. Deaf artists, performers, and professionals have government support to ensure their work is valued. In Canada, while there are efforts to promote Deaf arts and culture, they are often underfunded and require constant advocacy. Deaf-led projects frequently struggle to receive the same recognition and funding as hearing-led initiatives.

A Society That Understands Accessibility
In Finland, accessibility is seen as a shared responsibility, and society as a whole understands the importance of inclusion. Whether in public services, workplaces, or cultural institutions, there is a widespread understanding of Deaf needs. In Canada, accessibility is often treated as a favour rather than a right, and many Deaf people still have to fight for basic accommodations.

While Canada has made progress in Deaf rights and accessibility, Finland demonstrates a more comprehensive, well-funded, and legally supported approach. The difference is clear: in Finland, Deaf people are recognized as equal participants in society, while in Canada, accessibility often depends on whether an individual or organization is willing to provide it.

This comparison underscores the need for policy reforms in Canada to better support its Deaf communities, ensuring that barriers to access are removed and Deaf individuals can fully participate and contribute to society.

A Call for Change

Another issue I would like to highlight is theatre accessibility.

Theatre has long been a space for storytelling, expression, and inclusion, but when it comes to accessibility, are we truly breaking barriers – or unintentionally reinforcing them? The use of interpreters onstage, whether Deaf or hearing, is often seen as a solution for accessibility in theatre. However, is it really the best artistic choice or does it create a division between Deaf and hearing audiences? Instead of integrating sign language seamlessly into the performance, does it reduce it to an add-on, separate from the artistic experience? This debate challenges the assumptions behind interpreted performances and explores whether they truly serve Deaf audiences – or simply maintain the status quo.

This is a debate for another time and place, but what I will say now is this: Theatre has the power to transform perspectives, but true change demands dismantling the systemic barriers that continue to exclude Deaf voices. Allies in the hearing community must go beyond acknowledging these challenges – they must use their privilege to advocate for genuine accessibility and equity. For Deaf artists, representation isn't just about being heard – it's about being seen, understood, and valued.

Through my journey, I've learned that leadership isn't about having all the answers; it's about creating spaces where others can thrive. Together, we can build a world where Deaf artists no longer have to fight for a seat at the table but are celebrated for their unique contributions.

My story isn't just about overcoming barriers – it's a testament to resilience, community, and the transformative power of the arts. And it all started with one question: 'Why not me?'

Excerpt and Notes from *Prince Hamlet*
Why Not Theatre

HAMLET: To be, or not to be: that is the question,
Whether 'tis nobler in the mind to suffer
The slings and arrows of outrageous fortune,
Or to take arms against a sea of troubles,
And by opposing end them? To die: to sleep –
No more; and by a sleep to say we end
The heart-ache and the thousand natural shocks
That flesh is heir to, 'tis a consummation
Devoutly to be wish'd. To die, to sleep –
To sleep: perchance to dream: ay, there's the rub,
For in that sleep of death what dreams may come,
When we have shuffled off this mortal coil,
Must give us pause. There's the respect
That makes calamity of so long life.
For who would bear the whips and scorns of time,
The oppressor's wrong, the proud man's contumely,
The pangs of despised love, the law's delay,
The insolence of office and the spurns
That patient merit of the unworthy takes,
When he himself might his quietus make
With a bare bodkin? who would fardels bear,
To grunt and sweat under a weary life,
But that the dread of something after death,
The undiscover'd country from whose bourn
No traveller returns, puzzles the will
And makes us rather bear those ills we have
Than fly to others that we know not of?
Thus conscience does make cowards of us all;
And thus the native hue of resolution
Is sicklied o'er with the pale cast of thought,
And enterprises of great pith and moment
With this regard their currents turn awry,
And lose the name of action. – Soft you now!
The fair Ophelia! Nymph, in thy orisons
Be all my sins remember'd.

HAMLET: The question is: is it better to be alive or dead? (To be or not to be) Is it nobler to put up with all the nasty things that luck throws your way, or to fight against all those troubles by simply putting an end to them once and for all? Dying, sleeping – that's all dying is – a sleep that ends all the heartache and shocks that life on earth gives us – that's an achievement to wish for. To die, to sleep – to sleep, maybe to dream. Ah, but there's the catch: in death's sleep who knows what kind of dreams might come, after we've put the noise and commotion of life behind us. That's certainly something to worry about. That's the consideration that makes us stretch out our sufferings so long. After all, who would put up with all life's humiliations – the abuse from superiors, the insults of arrogant men, the pangs of unrequited love, the inefficiency of the legal system, the rudeness of people in office, and the mistreatment good people have to take from bad – when you could simply take out your knife and call it quits? Who would choose to grunt and sweat through an undiscovered country from which no visitor returns, which we wonder about without getting any answers from and which makes us stick to the evils we know rather than rush off to seek the ones we don't? Fear of death makes us all cowards, and our natural boldness becomes weak with too much thinking. Actions that should be carried out at once get misdirected, and stop being actions at all.

But *shh*, here comes the beautiful Ophelia. Pretty lady, please remember me when you pray.

OPHELIA: Good my lord,
How does your honour for this many a day?

HAMLET: I humbly thank you; well, well, well.

OPHELIA: My lord, I have remembrances of yours,
That I have longed long to re-deliver;
I pray you, now receive them.

HAMLET: No, not I;
I never gave you aught.

OPHELIA: My honour'd lord, you know right well you did;
And, with them, words of so sweet breath composed
As made the things more rich: their perfume lost,
Take these again; for to the noble mind
Rich gifts wax poor when givers prove unkind.
There, my lord.

HAMLET: Ha, ha! are you honest?

OPHELIA: My lord?

HAMLET: Are you fair?

OPHELIA: What means your lordship?

HAMLET: That if you be honest and fair, your honesty should admit no discourse to your beauty.

OPHELIA: Could beauty, my lord, have better commerce than with honesty?

HAMLET: No, not I;
transform honesty from what it is to a bawd than the
force of honesty can translate beauty into his
likeness: this was sometime a paradox, but now the
time gives it proof. I did love you once.

OPHELIA: Indeed, my lord, you made me believe so.

HAMLET: You should not have believed me; for virtue cannot
so inoculate our old stock but we shall relish of
it: I loved you not.

OPHELIA: Hello, my lord, how have you been doing lately?

HAMLET: Very well, thank you. Well, well, well.

OPHELIA: My lord, I have some mementos of yours that I've been meaning to give back to you for a long time now. Please take them.

HAMLET: No, it wasn't me. I never gave you anything.

OPHELIA: My lord, you know very well that you did, and wrote letters to go along with them, letters so sweetly written that they made your gifts even more valuable. Their perfume is gone now, so take them back. Nice gifts lose their value when the givers turn out not to be so nice. There, my lord.

HAMLET: Ha, ha! are you honest?

OPHELIA: Excuse me?

HAMLET: Are you beautiful?

OPHELIA: My lord, what are you talking about?

HAMLET: I'm just saying that if you're good and beautiful, your goodness should have nothing to do with your beauty.

OPHELIA: But could beauty be related to anything better than goodness?

HAMLET: Sure, since beauty's power can more easily change a good girl into a whore than the power of goodness can change a beautiful girl into a virgin. This used to be a great puzzle, but now I've solved it. I used to love you.

OPHELIA: You certainly made me believe you did, my lord.

HAMLET: You shouldn't have believed me, since we're all rotten at the core, no matter how hard we try to be virtuous. I didn't love you.

(63)

hmm... mem
alive   dead
     which better?
life (gun bullet) & (me)
bear with, face hit
     go through   or   cut-throat-grave † "sleep"
                         (hit face) heart ache
                         ↓ ⌐ ↓ fade away perfect!
                              sleep. die. plm (out of window)

                         dreaming... (eyes closed)
                                     eyes open.
                              what? not good...

me life suffer
(go thru ⅔) bullying.
(L→) system, gov't (R)
           no good!
people mean, love ♡ ↓ none.
(us) good people (you) mistreat
         who want that?
              better ⇗   cut wrist (blood dripping)
                         (relieved) (sleep)

hmm (point) -
not hard process   (point) death - scared...
    some prefer.. why?   once gone ⇝ explore
                         come back inform (me)
                              never...
                         (ooh..) go ahead cut wrist
                         go to heaven ↑ or ↓ hell.
                              (eek) which?
(process
 mistakes)?
                    passive?
         hmm...

ooh.. beautiful Ophelia!
   beautiful lady
      you pray, remember me...

Hamlet (1.p.o.v.)

→ How am I? well.. well...
→ No didn't give you letter...

→ you honest?
→ you beautiful?
→ I mean should beauty – honesty separate.

→ better separate
(1) beauty → honesty (2) (take over)
   fucking (2) become whore – whore
   (oh) go back can't.
   I did love you. ONCE

→ Believe me? No..
   everyone a) liars (both hands)
   I love you (no)

Taking Up Space in an Ableist World

In Conversation with April Hubbard

Award-winning artist and drag performer April Hubbard is a vibrant member of the East Coast theatre scene, with an extensive journey from mainstream, non-Disabled theatre toward her current practice in Disability and circus arts. April was a recipient of the 2025 Governor General's Performing Arts Awards. In this conversation with Debbie Patterson, April discusses the ways her disability has influenced her artistic practice and how her artistic practice has influenced her experience of disability.

Debbie Patterson: Could you first talk about your artistic practice?

April Hubbard: I started as a traditional theatre artist back in the early 2000s here in Nova Scotia, and at that point I was still appearing very able-bodied. But within the first probably five years of my career, I started to develop more of a limp and had to use forearm crutches. And at that point, I couldn't really hide my disability fully anymore. And at that point, the opportunities to be onstage completely dried up. I went from doing five to six shows a year to doing two shows over a seventeen-year period after I became openly Disabled, and both of those were because they needed a woman with a disability. So yeah, it was very obvious that I wasn't welcomed in the theatre world here in Nova Scotia as somebody who was visibly Disabled, to the point that I was going through the Dalhousie acting program and was asked to leave because I was told that my limp would be a distraction to the audience. So I kind of just hid behind the scenes for many years, but I kept being called back, wanting to be a part of the arts and wanting to be involved in some way. So I started volunteering, doing whatever, and as a result, became an arts administrator, even though that wasn't what I wanted to do – it was the only place that there was room for me.

In 2018 I was invited to be a part of a local workshop here in Halifax that was being led by Vanessa Furlong and Erin Ball of LEGacy Circus to teach instructors how to best interact with atypical bodies and Disabled bodies. They needed volunteers to sit in on the workshop and be the practice folks, and as soon as I touched the circus apparatus, I was in love, and that was my new way of expressing myself artistically. And that connected me with Vanessa, who has remained an important collaborator in my life and work.

During the pandemic, when everything was shut down and I was trying to find new ways of being artistic, I decided, after some conversations with a close friend, to try drag. So I've been performing under the name Crip Tease as a local drag artist.

DP: It's so interesting. Your journey is so much like mine: starting as an able-bodied theatre artist, and then developing a limp, and then that limp ... All the skills you have as a theatre artist – the vocal skills and text skills and being emotionally available – none of it matters. Fucking limp! It's cool that you found your way back in through circus.

AH: Circus is very much an art that centres the outsider, that celebrates the fact that we're all different and don't belong in all these ways, and kind of celebrates the other. So it seemed like the perfect way back, and circus was really an environment that seemed to celebrate my body – the fact that I could do things that others couldn't, and that my upper-body strength was really a cool thing in the circus – that I could do these tricks that most people who had been doing circus much longer couldn't, because I had the strength that they didn't from working my arms all the time as a wheelchair user.

DP: Are you willing to talk a bit about your disability?

AH: Certainly. I was born with spina bifida, although I never really had a chance to explore what that meant for me. In my youth it was something we didn't talk about and didn't explore at all: I kind of just pushed it aside and ignored it. And it wasn't until I was sixteen and I was walking down a flight of stairs at school one day. I heard a snap in my foot, and within a half-hour my foot had completely swollen out. It was a mystery; the doctors weren't really sure what had happened. I spent the next year on forearm crutches, and they were worried at that point, after a year, that I had done some damage to my hands and the nerves in my arms from using crutches for so long. So, they did a CT scan and, in one of the shots, saw a spinal cord tumour. So I got my diagnosis of tethered spinal cord completely by accident. They told me it was just temporary, and they'd fix it and then I'd go back to being like a 'normal' teenager. That didn't happen, and about five years later, I started to think, 'Yeah, this is going to shape who I am and affect every decision of my life and my day-to-day living. And I really have to start figuring out what that means for me, and I can't just keep ignoring the fact that other people see me as different and treat me differently. I also have to start looking at how this shapes who I am as a person, and begin seeing it as both a positive and a negative.'

DP: That's so interesting. I'm always interested in the difference between being a tourist in disability and being a lifer. And there really is a transition we go through when we buy into being a lifer.

AH: It lets you start moving forward.

DP: As long as you're a tourist, you're just waiting to get back to normal. You're stuck until you recognize, 'This is my normal.' In what ways have you found that process valuable?

AH: The first big change I noticed was just allowing myself to accept the help I needed. And that first came into my life in allowing myself to use a wheelchair. For about five years, I only used forearm crutches, even though I could only take a few steps, and I was really struggling to do even that, it was causing a lot of pain. But nobody had suggested to me using any other kind of mobility device. It was my parents who first suggested I use a wheelchair. And I said, 'Well, no, I can't use that. That's for somebody else – I'm not that bad.' And I was othering again and again. And it wasn't until my father went out one day and picked up a wheelchair and was like, 'You're going to try to use this.' And I realized, 'Oh, I actually can accomplish things I've wanted to do for so long.' And it was like a whole new world opened up to me. Then I had to start dealing with the whole question of what does this mean if I'm Disabled long-term? And that led me to looking for other people who were going through it, and talking to them and then finding the whole disability kinship as well, which really opened up a lot of new doors and windows in my life. Yeah, so there were a lot of little steps along the way to think about – 'What are my needs and what do I need to get through the day?'

DP: So how do you think your disability has shaped your artistic practice?

AH: My disability shaped my artistic practice in a lot of ways, but I think the most important has been to give myself permission to tell my own story. I think as women, we're encouraged to kind of stay in the background, to be meek and quiet and support the stories that are more important to be told. And then as a Disabled woman, that's amplified even more, so we don't have a right to tell our stories. So, with so many years of being pushed out of the theatre scene, it pushed me to the point of saying, 'I don't care anymore about what anybody else thinks. I have to speak up for myself, because nobody else is going to, and this story needs to be told.' So yeah, it gave me the courage to have a voice, not only for my own story, but also looking at the other stories around me that I felt needed to be told, whether that's amplifying BIPOC stories or trans stories. And if I'm given a small foot in the door, I'm going to push my way through and bring a bunch of other people with me and force them to listen.

I started to notice that even just in my arts administration career, not even as an artist, but I started to notice that when I showed up in a wheelchair at events, people wouldn't take me seriously unless I was dressed extra-professional, and as a result, I would always wear the fancy dress or the business suit to every event. And I kind of became known for that here in Halifax: that April dresses up to all these events. And people thought I was doing it just to kind of be artistic, to be fancy, but it was really because I realized I was being treated as the help that didn't matter.

The first time I really noticed it was at Halifax Fringe. One year I had an artist who came in and I met them in my fringe T-shirt and jeans, and they were treating me really, really horribly the whole time. And then a few days later, at one of the events, one of the other artists introduced me as the chair of the Halifax Fringe, and they treated me completely differently when I was dressed up, and it was like, 'Oh, this person matters now.' And I noticed that happening again and again, that I really had to present myself aesthetically as somebody who they thought mattered in order to be listened to at all and be heard.

DP: Wow, that's a real weird kind of ableism.

AH: Yeah, exactly.

DP: And do you think it's because you're a woman or because you're in a wheelchair?

AH: I think it's both. And I think one amplifies the other. I mean, I think part of it is we're just programmed not to listen to feminine voices as much in our society, and the big, booming male voices get the most attention. Also I'm viewed as more diminutive, more weak, more meek when I'm sitting in my manual chair, as opposed to a more imposing figure who may be standing next to me; as a result, whether it's conscious or not, I think a lot of people don't take my thoughts and my opinions quite as seriously.

DP: Yeah, which is also why circus would be so attractive: you just take up a lot of space in circus.

AH: Exactly. And I think that for all of us Disabled artists, the lesson we've had to learn, is how do we enter a room and claim that space and take that space and make sure people are going to listen to us?

DP: Do you think your art has informed the way you deal with your disability?

AH: Yeah, I think that talking about my disability in an artistic setting makes it feel safer for a lot of people. I consider myself both an artist and a disability advocate – both are big points of pride for me. But I'm very conscious of what messages I bring into an advocacy world and what messages I bring into an artistic world. Because I think people are more willing to listen when they're coming into an artistic space – to have their thoughts and perceptions challenged – whereas in an advocacy space, a lot of people can go into it with a more controversial approach, and as soon as their beliefs are challenged, the walls go up automatically. In an artistic space, I can plant seeds and maybe get a little bit further before they start to feel uncomfortable and those walls go up.

So I've found I can make it a little further in the conversation when I take an artistic approach rather than an advocacy approach. And that's been a real strength for me over the years – being able to get a lot of messages across as an artist that I wouldn't have otherwise through my advocacy. I think one definitely informs the other. And for me personally, anyway, I can't totally separate one from the next. All of my art is advocacy, because as soon as we put ourselves onstage as somebody with an atypical body – and for me, an atypical mind as well, because I identify as mad – that is a political statement. So one can't be completely separated from the next.

DP: Can you talk a bit about the importance of community in disability and in art?

AH: The community has been what's allowed me to keep going for so long and fight for so long, for so many years. When I found my space, through the arts, through circus, through drag, it really came with a built-in community, a support and a network of other people. And I could see behind the scenes whether they were ready to be openly Disabled or not. I could see other people fighting the same fight alongside me, and there were people to turn to when I had those horrible days when I just felt like it's never going to change or that there's never going to be any improvement, and nobody's listening to me. I knew who to turn to and who to lean on, and we could just come together and say, 'Okay, I need a break right now, but there's somebody else to take the torch and keep the fight going for a little while.' Because for so many years I felt like I'm the only one, and if I don't keep going, then nobody will keep this fight up. So when I could find that community, it made such a difference for me and gave me the courage to really keep fighting, and not only keep fighting for myself, but keep fighting for so many others.

For me, for so long too, I felt like – in Nova Scotia anyway – I was the only example of a Disabled performer who was openly out as Disabled. And as a result, people could point to me and say, 'Well, April came out, and all of her work disappeared, and she's been treated like crap, and she's only pulled out for the photo ops and then pushed back into the background to write the grants again and make it happen for everybody else, and we don't want that to happen to us, so we're not going to come out publicly as Disabled, as openly Disabled.' And I was kind of being used as a cautionary tale for many years. But I can now point to ten other people who are working openly as Disabled people in the arts and who are starting to build careers. It makes it all feel a little more worthwhile, because even though it felt like we were doing it alone for so many years, we can now see that interconnectedness and how we were all planting the seeds for one another and supporting one another. Whether we knew the other existed in the moment or not, we can see the path to the end and where it's led us now.

DP: Yeah, yeah, that's a powerful legacy. Do you want to talk about your decision to seek medical assistance in dying, or MAID?

AH: Definitely. So I put it off for a very long time. I always kind of knew in my adult life that, having a degenerative condition, I would probably get to the point where my quality of life didn't feel like it was tipping the scales and didn't feel like I was having enough of the positive anymore. So when I had my last relapse, which would have been in the fall of 2022, I spent about a year kind of wrestling with 'Is this just another bump in the road or is this actually approaching the end now?' And it wasn't until the summer of 2023 that I actually started talking to anybody in my life about applying for MAID. Then I put the application in around early fall of 2023.

At this point I'm actually approved for MAID. It's been a real safety net and a lifeline for me. I have the safety net of knowing that if things change tomorrow and I'm in a totally different situation and feel trapped, I have that way out now. It's my safety net, my escape zone, that I won't get stuck in the health care system and not be able to get out. I have this final treatment, and that's the way I see MAID – as a final treatment for me that is able to give me peace. And it has really allowed me to keep pushing and living life, even though I'm having a lot more symptoms that I thought would be past what I would be comfortable living with.

DP: That's really incredible. I've never heard anyone speak about MAID in that way: that it frees them to go further than they thought they would.

AH: And I do plan to push it for as far as I possibly can, until I know at my core that this is not a life I want to live anymore, and I'm ready to go. And I don't know when that will be, but I know now that I have the safety of knowing there's a way out, there's treatment for me in the end.

DP: Knowing that you've got that safety net, does that change the kind of art you want to do, the kind of stories you want to tell? Or does it influence it at all?

AH: I don't think that having MAID in place has shifted the type of stories I want to tell, the type of art I want to make, but it has given me the courage to be okay with burning bridges and taking more risk. For many years, I was always thinking about how much can I actually say and how much truth can I actually tell? Because I still need these allies, and I still need to follow this process, and I still need to play the game in a certain way to be accepted enough in mainstream performance spaces and be given a way in the door. But now I've kind of let go of all that, and I have the freedom to burn the bridges with the people who don't matter to me anymore, and to really put my time and attention to the people who do matter. And who have been there all along the way. And it's really given me a freedom to just be fully myself and not hold back in any way, and not have to play the game quite as much anymore, to just be one hundred percent authentic and myself.

DP: That's remarkable.

AH: Yeah. And one thing I've noticed, both in an artistic sense and just in the day-to-day, is it seems to give everybody else around me a freedom to be totally themselves, whether that's telling me secrets they've never told anybody – and some people will be very upfront about it, saying, 'I'm telling you because you're not going to be around here much longer anyway, so I feel I can tell you' – or just artistic collaborators being so much more free around me and open and honest and taking more risks. And it's been amazing to see everybody around me kind of experience that freedom alongside me, to be more of themselves and more authentic and just more artistic in their day-to-day lives as well, and it's been really, really awesome to witness.

DP: What do you mean by more artistic in their day-to-day lives – like just prioritizing joy and beauty rather than work?

AH: Yeah? I mean prioritizing the things that matter for them and the art they want to make. I think watching me approach my death – I've been very upfront about the fact that there are more projects I'd like to do that I kind of ran out of time for, that I won't get to do now, or at least won't get to do them in the way I wanted to do them originally. So, sharing that with the people around me has allowed them to take more artistic freedoms in their lives. But also I see other people around me have the freedom to just to talk more openly and share more freely about what they're feeling and not hold anything back. And I think that's been one gift that MAID has really given me. Because I'm open about the fact that I'm accessing MAID, nobody in my life has to be surprised by my death coming. They get the opportunity to say everything they want to and be totally upfront and have those moments with me while I'm here. And we can have all those beautiful conversations and beautiful interactions, and yes, they're hard and ugly and come with a lot of emotion, but there's such a freedom and beauty in that, and it's been great to see everybody around me really starting to cling to that more and live life more, more artistically.

DP: That's amazing. That's a huge gift you're giving the people around you.

AH: Yeah? And I mean, whether it's something as simple as I really like tulips, and before, I never had the time to stop and appreciate them, but this year I'm really going to appreciate them and bring them inside and surround myself with tulips while they're in season. Yeah, there have been a lot of beautiful moments like that that I've been able to witness.

DP: Is there anything else you want to say about your practice or your disability or the way these two things kind of serve each other in your life?

AH: For me, the biggest lesson I learned when I really connected with Disability Arts and Crip Arts was that for so many years, there was one way that I thought art had to be done, and it involved a lot of people and a lot of procedure. And when I really went into the Disability Arts world and worked with other Disability artists, the most important lesson I learned was that it was as much about the process as it was the end result. There were a lot of days, especially with circus, that my body just wasn't cooperating. And I'd go to rehearsal with Vanessa, and I just couldn't move and just had to lie on the mat and watch her rehearse. And I learned how that was as important a part of the process as me getting up in the air on the trapeze and flinging myself around.

It was all part of the learning and the community and the building and the creation. And if I have to create from my bed and tell a story that way instead, even though it may not be the original way I wanted to tell the story, there can be as much beauty as there could be from a full Shakespearean production that I put together with a whole group and put out onstage. Both have value and both are important and both deserve to be celebrated.

So yeah, I think the process is really important. I was reminded the most of that when Vanessa and I – we had applied for one final residency at the beginning of April to do a dance performance together, which we went into knowing it would be our final piece together. We were struggling in the early stages of rehearsal, and just nothing was clicking. We had all these ideas, but they weren't coming together, and they weren't showing themselves onstage the way we wanted them to. And as we were leaving rehearsal one day, really frustrated, we ran into another friend of ours from the dance community, and she said, 'Well, you guys always do this really cool described narration that's almost like poetry. Why don't you just write a poem that tells the story you want to say and not feel like you have to say it physically in the same way.' And from that moment on, it just clicked for us, and everything came together. And it was using that access that made the story unfold and made it so much deeper. It was a reminder that, okay, we need to go back to the process and why we're here – celebrating our partnership, going back to the roots of who we're doing this for, and highlighting the access measures first, and the rest will all fall into place. And it did, and as a result, it was one of our most amazing, powerful pieces.

- How do I ensure each actor's lines are translated from their meaning, rather than imposing my own interpretation?
- How is my signing as Horatio distinct from that of the other characters?

On top of all this, I also had to teach the actors their lines in ASL. Typically, an ASL coach would handle this, but since we discovered late in the process that Horatio would tell the entire story, there wasn't time to bring in an external coach. Teaching ASL isn't a one-size-fits-all process — you can't just hire someone in the middle of rehearsals and expect immediate success. The ASL coach must deeply understand the script, the actors, the director's vision, and how all these elements interact. Every actor is different; I had to study each one — how they move, how quickly they pick up signs, their depth of ASL fluency — and determine what was needed to make the story ultimately work.

Prince Hamlet Second Run (2019 - Canadian Tour)

By our second run of *Prince Hamlet* in 2019, everything elevated to another level. The same cast returned, and their ASL fluency had grown tremendously, allowing us to delve deeper into the script. I even refined my own translations to better match the evolving performances. Another major challenge I faced as a Deaf actor was trying to follow spoken English. Remember that everyone in the cast was hearing except for me. I had to ensure I knew exactly where they were in their lines – because if they missed a cue, chaos would follow. There were over one thousand cues I had to memorize. At times, actors forgot their lines or cues, and while I couldn't hear them, I instantly felt something was wrong. I call this my superpower (almost like my sixth sense). They often forgot their privilege of relying on sound, but I adapted and kept the performance on track. For me, *Prince Hamlet* wasn't just double the work – it was ten times the work.

Some of the audience feedback took me by surprise. Many hearing viewers were deeply moved by scenes that had no spoken dialogue –

especially my visual portrayal of Ophelia's drowning, which used neither ASL nor spoken English. Some even shared that my ASL helped them understand Shakespeare more clearly than they ever had before. Through this, I realized that the painstaking process of breaking down Shakespeare's lines for translation didn't just help me convey the text – it deepened my own understanding of his work.

Without that level of precision and analysis, true translation wouldn't be possible.

For many culturally and linguistically Deaf audience members, this was a groundbreaking experience – the first time they had ever seen a main character like themselves on a Canadian stage. Some had never even set foot in a theatre before, yet here they were, truly seeing themselves represented. They were able to sit in the audience and enjoy a three-hour performance free of barriers – something rarely available elsewhere. They witnessed ASL in a way they had never seen before; ASL onstage is not the same as everyday conversation. If Shakespeare is music to hearing people's ears, I wanted Shakespeare to be music to Deaf people's eyes. This show became a bridge, uniting audiences regardless of signing ability, allowing them to sit together and appreciate the depth and richness of storytelling – especially the profound friendship between Deaf Horatio and hearing Hamlet.

For us Deaf people, watching a show that is fully accessible is a fundamentally different experience than watching interpreters onstage, because of the way the story and emotions are conveyed. Here's how:

1. **Immersive experience:** When a show is fully accessible, it is designed to include all audiences from the very beginning – whether Deaf or hearing. This means sign language is integrated into the performance itself, rather than being an added layer on top. Deaf audience members can experience the narrative directly without having to focus on a separate interpreter. The sign language is part of the story, woven into the flow of the performance, creating a more natural, immersive experience for Deaf viewers.

Dancing Into Connection

In Conversation with Christopher DeGuzman

Actor and dancer Christopher DeGuzman is a core member of the Winnipeg-based Deaf mime troupe 100 Decibels. Acclaimed for their Deaf-led physical comedy, they have performed across Canada in productions with Theatre Projects Manitoba, the Canada Summer Games, and the Sound Off Festival Alberta. In conversation with Debbie Patterson, Christopher discusses his early artistic influences and his current practice, exploring how growing up without language nurtured his extravagant expressiveness.

Debbie Patterson: Christopher, I'd like to ask you to introduce yourself.

Christopher DeGuzman: For sure, happy to. I'm Christopher DeGuzman. I am thirty-eight years old, and I was born in the Philippines, and I identify as a Deaf individual; I became Deaf after birth.

We moved to Canada in 2010. The Society for Manitobans with Disabilities provided an immigrant program, and they had Deaf immersion classes. So Deaf immigrants would come to learn American Sign Language and English. And so that was actually how I gained knowledge of ASL and English.

DP: Wow, wow. So you didn't know ASL before 2010?

CD: Yeah, I didn't know it.

And it was Judith – she was one of my teachers who was teaching me ASL and English as well, and I was a bit of a goof – who was able to recognize the fact that I would play with American Sign Language signs, and I would play with the signs from Filipino Sign Language, I was able to incorporate them both. And it was actually her idea to – she kind of put it out there, like, 'What do you think about theatre?' Because I was a bit of a goof, and I was very creative. And so she put that idea forth, and she showed me a video of a person riding a bike. And she asked me to perform, you know, 'What does it look like to ride a bike?' and then I would figure out how to mime it. And she was able to connect me up with Shannon Guile, who was teaching mime to Deaf individuals. And so that's how I got involved with her and how I got my start in mime, with Shannon. She made that introduction for me. There was a group of five boys, it was a bit of a guys' group. The five of us got together just learning some real basics of mime, with Shannon as our teacher. And I found that I really took to it. I really enjoyed it, and it was something I seemed to be pretty good at. And then Joanna Hawkins joined the group, and some of the guys left, which, eventually, as we honed our skills and practised, led to our mime troupe, 100 Decibels. With me, Joanna, and Jordan Sangalang.

The first time we did a performance was at Fringe Festival, and I was so, so nervous. I remember that moment of how nervous I was. I remember Shannon was learning sign language, and I just have such fond memories of how she would try to sign the sign for 'Are we ready to go?' – but she would sign the sign that actually means grey, the colour grey. I just have such fond memories of the fact that she used to make these slip-ups in her sign language because she was still learning, but she was trying so hard.

That was really the first time I did any sort of live performance to a live audience, public audience, where I could actually see that what we were doing was having an impact on them. There was a lot of emotion. People were laughing, and they really took to it. So I really enjoyed that.

DP: Had you been involved in mime or theatre back home?

CD: I was, you know, a pretty athletic person in secondary school and so was really interested in dance as well. I attended a college where I'm from. The CAP College for the Deaf in Manila.

I ended up taking two majors, economics/technology and also business management, while I was there – accounting and things of that nature – and got a certificate for both of those programs. But I really, really got into dance, and I really loved dancing as a younger person. And so I also took dance while in college.

DP: So your way into theatre was through dance first.

CD: Absolutely, I did a lot of hip hop, jazz dance, cultural dancing as well, like traditional Filipino dancing.

DP: Wow, I didn't know that about you, Christopher, that's so cool.

CD: I do have some residual hearing, but I also use the vibrations, not that I can understand the lyrics of the songs, but I am able to really help identify the beat with the music, and so I'm able to kind of pick it up in both ways, but I can never really hear the lyrics.

DP: Do you still consider yourself a dancer, or do you perform as a dancer?

CD: I mean, I haven't done much lately, because of a lot of barriers.

DP: Can you tell me about all the things you've worked on in the last couple of years with 100 Decibels?

CD: We were a part of a Deaf festival: SOUND OFF in Edmonton, or Calgary and Edmonton. We've done that now for several years.

We were flown out to Calgary to do the eightieth anniversary of the Calgary Association of the Deaf, and they hired us to come and do a performance later in that same year. Then we went to Toronto to Buddies in Bad Times.

In Winnipeg we've done Zoo Lights. And we did another piece that was part of a larger group called *Knock Knock Ginger* during the lockdown with Theatre Projects Manitoba. And then the Canada Summer Games at the Forks, and a bunch of shows with Sick + Twisted Theatre. And I really love working with everybody – hearing, Deaf, Disabled, or not. I've really enjoyed working with Sick + Twisted, and the experiences I've gained from that, it's been incredible.

DP: You were in Europe recently, weren't you? Could you talk about what those experiences were?

CD: We went to take a mime workshop at the International School of Dramatic Corporeal Mime in Paris. We went to France to do a mime workshop as a collective.

DP: Was that a workshop for Deaf artists?

CD: That workshop that we took in France was for Deaf and hearing individuals, but it was put on by a professional organization. It was incredible. And they were very welcoming to have us there. And after we were there, we actually attended a Deaf theatre festival called Clin d'Oeil, which happened to be running in the same week.

DP: What was a highlight?

CD: Just being in such a huge crowd of other performers and Deaf people – the environment, the music was blaring, everything was on high, you could see everybody signing. The party lasted three days straight. It never stopped. It was exhausting, but it was an incredible, incredible experience.

DP: When you're onstage, is it a different experience for you if there are lots of Deaf people in the audience?

CD: The first time I really ever experienced having an audience is in Canada, and those audiences are sometimes a mixture Deaf and non-Deaf. And honestly, for me it's the same. It's incredible. I enjoy having both Deaf people in the audience or having non-Deaf people in the audience. They both give me the rush of performing onstage. And I feel the same way, no matter who is in the audience.

DP: Could you talk a bit about how having a performance practice enriches your life? What effect does being a performer have on your day-to-day life?

CD: I was a pretty shy kid, and I didn't really want to socialize with other kids, other hearing kids, but my grandmother really helped me to come out of my shell. She connected me to dance. She's the one who really got me into it, and kind of forced me into it, and that allowed me to make friends, socialize, allowed me to make connections. Dance was the thing that really allowed me to break through that, helping me have that confidence to develop my skills and move forward. I think that's really what's led me to be the person I am now – because of that ability, I could break out of that shell. Getting involved in dance has led to other things. I was able to be part of comedy and develop these friendships and make those connections and banter with other kids. It actually led me to feel confident and gave me such happiness.

DP: You're a brilliant comedian. How did you get to be so funny?

CD: You know the old cartoon *Tom and Jerry*? It was one of my favourite cartoons as a kid, and I just loved that comedic style and that humour. And it was one of the things that affected my ability to develop that skill as well. I think having that ability to learn dance, having that connection with comedy, and knowing the cartoon example, like *Tom and Jerry* – those three things have really led to how I formed what I do as my practice. And those three things, I think, were the largest influences that I had in my performance.

DP: That's so cool.

CD: I can be a dancer and I can be comedic. I can bring all these things to the table when I do it. And that's kind of me in a nutshell.

DP: You *are* a bit of a nut.

CD: I'm creative, and I'm able to bring in comedy with a creative mindset. And mime is also something that really lends itself well to comedy and allows me to really express myself. I've really enjoyed being able to use those as my outlets, and that provides me with a lot of joy. Same with getting involved in Sick + Twisted and the cabarets or the different shows we've done that have given me a lot of happiness and joy.

DP: Well, you give joy to the audience with your performance.

CD: Oh, I don't know. I mean, I just do my best.

DP: So you say you were a shy kid. I always thought you were probably the class clown.

CD: I wasn't. I was incredibly shy, just a very shy kid growing up.

DP: Did you see much theatre or mime when you were a kid? Did you see any live performance, or were there any live performers who had an impact on you?

CD: Not any sort of formal things. I didn't ever have the chance to go, but I did attend local festivals in my area, smaller festivals that would have dancers. So I was able to see that type of thing once in a while, not frequently – but nothing in an actual, formalized theatre. I was able to see some when I attended college later. But otherwise, not so much. But when I moved to Canada, it was an eye opener. There were so many more things I was able to partake in, just in terms of festivals and shows, and everything after I moved to Canada was much more frequent.

DP: I feel like it's hard to imagine doing something if you don't see someone like you doing it. I find it really inspiring when I meet an artist who finds a way to do the work, even though there are so many barriers in the way, and there are no models, there's no one showing you how to do it, and you just kind of figure it out.

CD: Yeah, no, it's true. When I was growing up in the Philippines, you know, we didn't have access to interpreters. Everything that was spoken was not accessible to me. So it's not like I could partake in that way. And so I just kind of ignored it, right? Whereas my grandma would want me to go, you know, check out the dancing. But as soon as they would go to something where somebody was talking, I was like, 'Well, there's no interpreting, there's no captioning, there's no sort of access for me.' So that was quite a huge barrier, right? And I didn't really want to do that type of stuff, because what was the point, right?

There was nothing that made it accessible until I was in high school, at a school for the Deaf, and it was finally a place where I could connect with other people who were like myself, right? That was the first time I had that sort of experience where the teachers were not Deaf, but they would have an interpreter. And I was like, 'Oh, I didn't even realize,' you know, and I really liked how that changed things for me, and how I was able to kind of communicate and follow along in class, whereas prior to that, all I had been met with were barriers. Right? School was very difficult for me because I didn't have interpreters, I didn't have language until I went to that high school. It was really the first time that I saw myself able to do something. Prior to that, there was really not a lot of exposure. And my family also had never met any other Deaf people until I brought them to my high school, where they saw me signing. Because there's nobody else in my family who's Deaf. I'm the only one. I'm the only person. When I brought my family to the high school, the Deaf school, it was the first time they had met other Deaf people, or seen people signing in that type of environment. And I did most of the teaching of sign language to my family. I mean, because Filipino Sign Language is totally different, right?

My family would do home signs, we would gesture. We would communicate in our own way, but I would use the Filipino Sign Language to chat with other people who also knew that, but primarily any time I would communicate with my family or my relatives, we would use a home-based sign that was not based in Filipino Sign Language.

DP: You invented your own sign language with your family.

CD: Yeah, exactly.

DP: Wow. So you didn't learn any other sign language until you were in high school.

CD: That's right. And in terms of Filipino Sign Language and Tagalog, they're very similar in terms of the order of the grammar of the language. But FSL and ASL are very different. So it was really difficult: I had learned FSL, knew that language, but then when I came to Canada I had to learn ASL, and it was a totally different grammar system and sign language.

DP: Would you say your first language was the language you invented with your family?

CD: Yeah, yeah, it's very gestural, right? I would say primarily I communicated with my grandmother. I mean, my mother passed, and my father moved to the U.S. for work, but I grew up in the Philippines with my grandmother as caregiver, and so that's primarily why most of my communication was with my grandmother.

DP: Okay, last question: What is your gift to the world through your art?

CD: I think I want to give what I can to future generations so that children of today can grow up and develop and have the experiences and the exposures I may have not had, but to provide that to future generations.

DP: Do you hope your son becomes a performer?

CD: One hundred percent! I would love for him to grow a personality like that. I can share those things with him. I feel like it'll happen. I think it will.

DP: I think so too. Do you have anything else you want to say about your work as a performer? Any words of advice to other performers?

CD: I want to make sure I'm focusing on my work, but also focusing on my son, and able to have a good life balance, and I look forward to the future performances we'll have together.

This interview was conducted on Zoom with the support of ASL interpreter Cindy Boscow and Deaf interpreter Joanna Hawkins.

Conclusion

Alex Bulmer

As co-editor, I'm trying to craft a fitting and meaningful conclusion to this anthology, one that honours the artists and this collection of their diverse work. It's proving to be difficult. There is no definitive end to the voices and creativity expressed across these pages. The true nature of 'collection,' which is to gather rather than complete, seems incongruous with conclusions. So instead of seeking an end, I'll offer some personal reflection.

I am struck by what is both distinctive and shared across chapters: the unique and transformative imagination of each artist and the collective pursuit of care, humanity, and belonging. This might be a definition of excellence.

I am truly grateful to all the artists for their genuine, thoughtful, and generous contributions. Each artist's capacity to evolve and travel artfully through the unknown is profound. After working for thirty-five years as a Blind artist and Disability theatre–maker, I realize that time has not provided resolutions but has instead revealed deeper complexities and new dimensions. Disability Art is an ever-unfolding journey, a limitless exploration that defies the expectation of ever reaching a conclusion.

The full editorial team and I felt strongly that art should remain the central focus for this anthology. It was suggested that I might offer a full text of my unpublished play *Perceptual Archaeology (or How to Travel Blind)* as my chapter contribution. Initially I hesitated. I was concerned that it might be too specific to my experience, but considering we were encouraging each contributor to give their unique voice to the collection, I re-examined the text. Together, Debbie Patterson and I noted themes of travel, the unknown, imagination, and interdependence within the play, and agreed that these also resonate across the book. As a result, in lieu of a conclusion, what follows is the full play text as first produced in Toronto in 2023 by Fire and Rescue and Crow's Theatre. I'm honoured to publish my work alongside so many brilliant creators and to be celebrated within our vibrant and transformative community.

Thank you for reading our anthology. I hope you've found some treasure within these pages.

Perceptual Archaeology (or How to Travel Blind)
Alex Bulmer

Written and performed by Alex Bulmer
Directed by Leah Cherniak
First co-produced by Fire and Rescue Arts and Crow's Theatre, June 2023

Cast

Alex: A Blind traveller
Enzo: Alex's line feeder and stage assistant

As the audience enters the space, they are given a small stone.

The lights dim. Enzo enters and delivers a live pre-show audio description.

ENZO: Good evening. The theatre space we are in is rectangular in shape. Most of you are sitting along the length of the room, but a few of you are sitting along the shorter sides facing in toward the centre of the stage.

There are two of us in this production: Alex Bulmer, who wrote the travel essays this show is based on, and me, Enzo Massara – I'm the line feeder. Alex is a white woman with short light brown hair. She wears a red corduroy jacket, blue jeans, and burgundy lace-up boots. I'm a white man with dark, curly brown hair and a beard. I'm wearing a dark blue T-shirt, khaki pants, and sneakers.

The set for this show includes a ladder, an orange chair, a small round table, a small blue sofa, a green wooden travelling chest, and a tall bar table with wineglasses. In the performance, some set pieces will stand in for other things. For example, the sofa is also airplane seats.

In the middle of the stage, close to the audience, is a microphone stand with a cordless microphone.

Lastly, in the corner of the room, opposite from where you all entered, is my line-feeding station. This is where I will be for most of the show. Now I'm going to leave the room and go get Alex.

Enzo and Alex enter.

ENZO: Door opening toward you and on the left.

ALEX: Thank you.

ENZO: And you're at the mic.

ALEX: Hello, everyone. Hi, everyone! Okay, so about forty people. Practically Roy Thomson Hall.
I'm Alex Bulmer. I'm here with a nice man named Enzo.

ENZO: Yes, I'm the nice man.

ALEX: As you heard, Enzo is the line feeder, which means he will be speaking my text through a microphone that goes into this little earbud, here in my left ear. Is it okay if I mention …

Alex whispers to Enzo.

ENZO: Yes.

ALEX: Enzo is a gutsy guy; he's never done anything like this before?

ENZO: Right. Do we need to explain why I'm feeding the lines into your ear?

ALEX: No. Just head over to your station. Have fun.

ENZO: Okay, off to my station.

ALEX: Thank you for coming tonight for my talk called *Perceptual Archaeology (or How to Travel Blind)*. A rumination in five parts.

ENZO: Sorry, Alex, can I just check that the headset thing is working?

ALEX: Yes.

ENZO: Can you hear me, blah blah.

ALEX: Blah blah. Yes, I can hear you. A rumination in five parts. Just to say, feel free to respond any time. Snap your fingers, stomp your feet, and of course laugh. It's nice to know you're still here. Okay, here we go, let's talk.

Part One.

What is it like to travel blind?

A question I asked myself in the summer of 1996, while swimming in a pool in Los Angeles.

The years leading up to this moment in L.A. were turbulent. I was losing my sight. By age nineteen, I was sitting on people in movie cinemas, walking into trees, and, rather than driving my motorcycle across country roads, I drove across ditches. Doesn't every teenager do that?

By age twenty-one, a close friend of mine named Winkie thought there was something more serious going on here. So, on her encouragement, I booked myself into an eye clinic. On October 8, 1987, I walked into a Toronto hospital.

The appointment started at 8:30 a.m. in a small room with a team of doctors looking into my eyes.

Hours were filled with tests: colour cubes, flashing lights, endless drops. With a sleep shade over sore and dilated pupils, I listened while the doctors told me I had a genetic condition called retinitis pigmentosa and would be blind in five to fifty years. *(Alex continues in gibberish)* A genetic condition called Retinosas Pigmerstshna bilderfifeltufleus ...

The statement was delivered in spoken English, but it might as well have been gibberish. It was science fiction; it was someone else's script.

Back in the waiting room, my pupils finally returned to 'normal.' At 3 p.m. I left the hospital. I looked intently at everything. The light was bright, with only a dusting trace of white clouding the otherwise soft blue sky.

There were garden pots, pink-and-white-uniformed hospital staff, some standing, some sitting, some eating brown sandwiches. I could see. I could see. I could see.

Nine years later, the unthinkable warrant on my sighted future was becoming a reality.

And now, I give you exhibit A: the white cane.

This bright and beautiful mobility tool. One hundred and fifty centimetres of aluminum and fibreglass. It changed everything.

And it changed everything.

On sidewalks, parents would gasp, grab their children, and practically hurl them across the street to avoid me.

Taxis sped off when I approached the door. You think my cane's gonna pee on your back seat.

Enzo laughs.

Thank you, Enzo. Little guide-dog joke.

In 1996, alone one afternoon in my one-room Toronto apartment, I called my friend Winkie. She was living in Los Angeles at the time.

I told Winkie that I was struggling, that I hadn't left my apartment for over a week. I was scared. She said: 'Get on a plane, come to L.A., stay as long as you need.'

I told Winkie: 'No, I can't do that.'

Five minutes after hanging up the phone, I booked myself a flight to L.A. and a room in the airport hotel. I didn't tell Winkie. If I was going to escape the shrinking walls around me, I'd need to do it on my own. If something went wrong – Winkie was a phone call away.

August 1996.

Toronto to Los Angeles.

From a one-room apartment to outer space.

On my first day in L.A., I asked the hotel staff for some instructions to get to the outdoor pool.

I walked outside, using my cane to feel for the end of hard and the beginning of liquid.

My hand reached to confirm I had found *(feels the mic stand)* water.

Putting my cane aside, I sat on an edge and lowered myself into the pool.

Once in it, I realized I had no idea of its size, shape, or depth.

Reaching out, I felt for the pool wall – *(feels the mic stand)*

And started to swim.

I traced the wall with my hand

swimming – around.

I found cracks in the concrete, chunks missing …

I discovered filters and flaps.

Swimming,

I noticed the lap slap of water against the pool edge – it shifted to a hollow sound by

… the ladder.

Swimming,

I heard a lap echo slap beneath the diving board.

As I swam around … and around …

I came to understand …

the pool shape

was

that

of a kidney bean –

round at one end and more narrow at the other.

I discovered the pool, gradually, gathering pieces that, with the immediacy of sight, would have been eclipsed by the whole. *(Alex taps the mic)*

I bobbed in the water – making waves

And listening as they slapped against the edge of the pool. *(Alex stops tapping)*

Over there.

And over there

And I am here.

I listened …

Over there

And over there

And I am here.

Here within this particular collection of sounds and textures, this pool.

A shape of place emerged.

When place exists, I exist.

Going blind – from that moment these two words held new meaning. Going blind had been a fraying rope, a loss of presence and awareness.

Now, in this pool, this going blind felt like potential, a becoming – becoming a sensory mathematician, a perceptual archaeologist.

I bobbed in the water, feeling and listening. I decided that one day I would be a blind travel writer.

Alex takes out mic, stays centre stage.

Several years after the L.A. pool, while trying to be blind and have a quality of life and work within Canada, I could see the writing on the wall. Well, no. I could hear the sound of many doors closing.

I had a few blind friends in other countries. I knew there were less disabling places to live and work.

So, in 2004 I left Canada. And moved to London, England.

With no visual memories of the city, I relied entirely, and permanently, on my other senses. By age thirty-four, I felt I had shed my sighted past and finally found a future.

In 2012, while swimming off the coast of England, I thought about my big idea in the L.A. pool, to be a blind travel writer, and wondered how could I finally make this happen. Enzo?

ENZO: Yes, Alex.

ALEX: What do we do when we wonder?

ENZO: Um, we google?

ALEX: Yes, Enzo! We google. I typed three words into my search engine: 'blind travel writing.' And the first thing that came up was from the nineteenth century. The nineteenth century! The name of a British navy officer turned blind travel writer named James Holman.

The Wikipedia page about him was full of Royal Society this and that, which inspired a yawn. But then I found a section that intrigued me. Well, no, actually, it pissed me off.

Blind James Holman was, for a brief time, the most acclaimed travel writer in the world. *(Alex starts to pace)* He published many, many books. But other travel writers, sighted travel writers, disqualified his writing because, quote, 'no blind person could possibly document travel with any accuracy or validity,' end quote. Most of his books were therefore destroyed.

ENZO: Shit.

ALEX: Enzo, you just said 'shit.'

ENZO: Yes, sorry, Alex.

ALEX: No, no, it was shit. It was shitty shit shit.

And that shitty shit got my attention. I searched for whatever remaining James Holman writing I could find. I would bring this nineteenth-century blind traveller back to life. And I thought, that's the hook. Twenty-first-century Alex and nineteenth-century James, a tale of two blind travellers, across two hundred years of time, and hundreds of miles of space. I'd go where he travelled.

The idea had it all – history, geography, travel, blindness, and fury! How could it not get funding! And guess what, Enzo?

ENZO: You got funding.

Alex sings 'Don't Fence Me In,' adding in her new lyrics.

> Just let me be, happily, as I wander and I sing- a-ling-a-ling
> On my ol' pony he's called Tony, and like me he can't see a frickin' thing
> I wanna roll in the grass with my better senses
> Shake a little ass as the day commences
> I like open fields but I don't like fences
> Don't fence me in

> I'll wander cheerily, maybe blearily, always queerly as I sing-a-ling-a-ling
> On my ol' pony, he's called Tony, and like me he can't see a fuckin' thing
> I wanna roll on the ground with my better senses
> Shake my ass around as the day commences
> Get me to a field, let me take some chances
> Don't fence me in

ALEX: I got funding! And planned my trip. I'd travel across Germany, Italy, and France. For eight weeks.

> Discovering, on my own, taking risks. And it did occur to me that perhaps having a sighted someone in the background might be a sensible option. So I asked my good friend Michael if he would travel with me – and he said yes.

Banjo continues.

> So, on October 8, 2014, seventeen years after my big idea in the L.A. pool, I left London on my way to Germany, on my way to become a blind travel writer.

Alex walks toward the sofa. She sits and folds her cane.

> Part Two – London to Freiberg.
> Our plane was late.
> Michael and I sat by the gate.
> I was nervous and excited about what was ahead – stepping into nowhere. Well – stepping into somewhere.

Boarding call announcement and then sounds of embarkment.

> At two-thirty we boarded the plane. Michael put my bag up overhead.

Sound of the overhead closing.

> Thank you.

Sound of seat belt.

    Seat belt.

RECORDED VOICE OF FLIGHT ATTENDANT: 'Ladies and gentlemen, please observe our safety instructions – if breathing becomes a problem, an oxygen mask will hang above you, etc.'

ENZO: Alex, can I describe what you were doing? It looked so good.

ALEX: Yes.

ENZO: So, Alex was listening intently to the flight attendant when she talked about the airbag.

ALEX: I take aviation safety very seriously, Enzo.

ENZO: And then she leaned back when the plane was taking off.

ALEX: I take theatrical mime very seriously, Enzo.

ENZO: So cool.

ALEX: You know I went to theatre school, Enzo.

ENZO: I auditioned but didn't get in.

ALEX: I'm really sorry. We need to get back to the airplane.
    I sat next to Michael. He was listening to music under headphones.
    I listened to James Holman writing.
    I poked Michael. Michael, listen to this. 'Blind James Holman climbed volcanoes. Active volcanoes!'
    Michael said, 'Hmm hmm,' and went back to his music. I went back to Holman.
    Michael, Michael. The guy climbed ships, the masts of ships, to the top, grabbed on to rope, and swung out over the sea.
    Michael said, 'Wow,' and went back to his music. I listened to more Holman.

I poked Michael. Michael, James Holman wrote, quote: 'I seek information and momentum, not safety and protection.' End quote.

Information and momentum, I think I seek that too.

Michael was happy for me, then went back to his music.

Sound of plane landing.

We landed. Had a beer in the airport to celebrate, then set off in a taxi to Freiburg.

We pulled up to our Airbnb, and Michael said our hostess Danielle was waving.

Alex waves.

I waved back. Bit silly really, kind of a one-way street.

Alex stands with cane.

I stepped out of the taxi and listened for audio clues of this new world. Over there, voices chatting several feet away; over there, the distant sound of a street musician; way over there, a dog. And not a single sound of an automobile. No cars blocking my hearing view.

(With cane) That night we walked the city. Danielle pointed out the highlights of Freiburg –

'There's the Minster, that's the oldest hotel in Germany, that's a shoe store, there's the stone archway, that's a wine bar, a mosaic, a shoe store, a bridge, a shoe store, the river, a shoe store, a mosaic, a brewery, a shoe store, a wine bar, a mosaic …'

The above loops.

Most of this had little meaning to me. Merely a list of words. Spoken over an hour. Into absence.

ALEX: Enzo.

ENZO: Yes, Alex.

ALEX: Can you please put a pillow on the chest, which will soon become the bed?

    Michael and I went back to our Airbnb …

Enzo sets the pillow.

    That night I stood in my room, I felt the walls, felt the door frame. I felt as if the world had disappeared.

Alex sits.

    There was no geography, no architecture, no here versus there …
    When there's nothing out there, there's nothing here.
    My chest, my shoulder, my feet.
    I reached out.
    I felt the mattress, the bed frame, the pillow.
    I felt my shoulder, my chest, my feet, the mattress, the pillow.
    I'm disappearing. Enzo?

ENZO: Yes, Alex.

ALEX: I'm going to take a little break.

ENZO: Oh, really? Are you really going to lie down?

ALEX: Yes.

Alex lies down on the bed.

ENZO: Okay. Do you need anything from me?

ALEX: Could you take over for a bit? Say the text out loud.

ENZO: Ummmm.

ALEX: Just read the text out loud. You'll be fine.

ENZO: Umm … sure.

    Okay. Enzo here. So, this next bit goes back to the nineteenth-century blind guy James Holman. While climbing Mount Vesuvius …

ALEX: Oh no, skip that bit, please. Go to the part with his writing, when he asks what's the point.

ENZO: Okay. What's the point of … Yup.

In 1822, James Holman wrote:

'I am constantly asked, and I'll answer it once and for all, what's the use in travelling for one who can't see? Does every traveller see all that they describe? Is not every traveller obliged to depend upon others for a great proportion of the information they collect? Works of art and the picturesque in nature are shut out from me. Perhaps this affords a stronger zest for curiosity, a closer examination of details than would be satisfied by first impressions seen through the eyes.

'Freed from being misled by appearances, I am compelled to collect information, which other travellers dismiss at first sight.' That's so good.

Alex sits up.

ALEX: It's so, so, so good.
I've got this now!

Alex stands on the bed.

Break time is over!
Day two in Freiburg. We are going to the Schlopssberg.

ENZO: Where?

ALEX: The Shlotsberg. *(recording: 'Schlossberg')* The Shlotsberg. *(recording: 'Schlossberg')* The Schlossberg.

On our second day in Freiberg, I made a strategic decision, in response to the panic I felt the night before. I asked Michael to walk me to a part of the Black Forest known as the Schlogssberg.

Alex pronounces it incorrectly. A recorded digital voice corrects her. This game repeats until …

A big hill. Enzo, would you please stand with me here on the big hill, which is actually the bed, which is actually the chest.

Perceptual Archaeology (or How to Travel Blind) | 221

ENZO: Sure.

Enzo walks over to Alex by the bed.

ALEX: You can play Michael.

ENZO: Really?

ALEX: You're an actor.

ENZO: Okay, I'm Michael.

Alex puts her arm out and accidentally hits Enzo and apologizes.

ALEX: I gave Michael my hand … and asked him to point at the various sites that we'd seen the day before.

Enzo points Alex's arm in different directions.

ENZO: The river, the Minster, the bridge, the mosaic, the stone archway.

Enzo lets go of Alex's arm.

ALEX: I'll do it now. The bridge, the river, the Minster …

ENZO: No, move your arm and point just to the right.

ALEX: The Minster, mosaics, the stone archway.

ENZO: And the Airbnb is just there.

ALEX: Oh, I thought it was over there.

ENZO: No. *(Enzo moves Alex's arm)*

ALEX: Through an understanding of here versus there, this versus that, a shape of place emerged. When place exists, I exist.

ENZO: That's wild and cool.

ALEX: Blind people are wild and cool. All two billion of us. Michael and I left the Schlossberg and visited the Minster. The Minster is the name of a very old, very large cathedral in Frieburg.

A digital recording corrects her pronunciation of Freiburg.

> Let's go.

Alex jumps off the chest and they walk.

> I used to think it was called a Munster, but Enzo googled it and told me that Munster is actually a kind of cheese.

ENZO: We're at the door.

ALEX: Here we are at the door, the big heavy doors of the Minster Munster. Michael, aren't they big heavy doors?

ENZO: Am I still Michael?

ALEX: Yes.

ENZO: Wow, what big heavy doors.

ALEX: We opened the big doors of the Minster. Oh, my goodness, more doors.

They leave the performance space and enter the theatre lobby.

> Wow! Can you hear that echo?

ENZO: Um, yes.

ALEX: It's such a huge space.

ENZO: It's huge. And oh, look at that beautiful, ornate, gold-plated table.

ALEX: It's called an altar.

ENZO: Oh, look at that gold-plated altar. And so many carvings and …

ALEX: Michael, listen to that sound. I think I hear a choir singing. Do you hear a choir?

ENZO: Yes. A choir.

ALEX: Let's find the choir. Excuse me, have you seen a choir walk by?

Alex talks to whoever is in the lobby.

PERSON: No.

ALEX: Do you work here?

The conversation continues as an improvisation. Eventually, Alex asks Enzo to go back into the theatre space.

>Is the audience still here?

ENZO: They are.

ALEX: It's a miracle, you can go back to your line-feeding station.
Could I have a round of applause, please?

Applause.

>Thank you. Hey! It's a choir!! Enzo, I found the choir! And what a good-looking bunch of singers you are ... says the blind one. And hey, I hear the organist, Neha, in the corner. Hi, Neha!
>Okay, let's do what choirs do – have a singalong. Don't worry, I can feel the dread in your faces. It'll be fine.
>Neha, could I have an A, please?

Sound of A on an organ.

>Hummmmmm. Hello, choir. Hmmm. If you were born between January 1 and July 31, please would you now hum with me. Hmmm. Please continue. Make sure you remember to breathe.
>Neha, could I have a D, please?
>Hmmmm. If you were born between July 31 and December 31, please hum this note with me.

The pre-recorded sound of a choir joins in.

>If you were never born, please hum this note with me.

> Keep humming and remember to breathe. If you stop breathing, your oxygen mask will drop from above. Please put your oxygen mask on first and then help the person next to you.
>
> Please keep humming.

The audience hums together.

> And ... STOP.

The sound of a beautiful Minster choir continues to fill the space.

> Wow! Listen to that.
> Within an acoustic horizon of voices,
> I moved through the Minster,
> Tracing its stone walls
> Discovering carvings and pillars
> Turning space into place.
> Thank you for humming.
> When there's something out there, there's something here.

Alex puts a hand on her chest.

> Enzo, I need to get to the ladder, which will become the restaurant.

ENZO: I'll take you.

ALEX: Thank you – No, wait, I have a better idea. How about I'll try to find it ... When I get closer, you say, 'Yeah,' and if I go the wrong way, you say, 'Boo.'

ENZO: Oh yeah, like hot and cold.

ALEX: Yes. Ready, I'm going.

Enzo 'boos' and 'yeahs' Alex to the ladder. She accidentally knocks off a trick glass of wine that is attached by a string.

> Yeah, it's the ladder – Oh no, I spilled my wineglass – But look! Not a drop left the glass! How lucky.

Perceptual Archaeology (or How to Travel Blind)

Restaurant sounds.

> That evening, Michael and I had dinner with two blind people, Vivian and Henrik.

Sound recording corrects her pronunciation.

> Henrik – Henrik. Both from Frieburg.

Sound recording corrects her pronunciation of Freiburg.

> Oh, for God's sake.
> Hey, Enzo, I've got an idea.

ENZO: What?

ALEX: I think we should do this next bit together. There's a microphone over there.

ENZO: Got it.

ALEX: Go for it.

ENZO: Okay. So, as you wrote, Vivian and Henrik were already in the Italian restaurant when Michael and I arrived.

ALEX: They were already there.

ENZO: Vivian approached us with striking confidence –

ALEX: Such elegance.

ENZO: And an unusually elegant handshake.

ALEX: I'm charmed already.

ENZO: Henrik offered the more traditional blind hand-hop, arms out, hands flapping.

ALEX: *(waving her arms around)* Nice to meet you, nope, nice to meet you, oops, nice to, over, up, sorry …

ENZO: Over a meal with pastas, antipastos, and red wine –

ALEX: A few too many glasses.

ENZO: We covered the subjects of night life, work opportunities, dating,

ALEX: dating,

ENZO: lack of support –

ALEX: Sounds familiar.

ENZO: Henrik founded a blind cultural centre called Dark Oasis.

ALEX: Dark Oasis – sounds like a thrash band.

ENZO: Henrik's work has prevented many blind people from becoming isolated or voiceless.

ALEX: Go, Henrik. Go, Henrik.

Italian music starts.

ENZO: Vivian spoke passionately about the Paralympics.

ALEX: A bronze!!

ENZO: Earlier that morning, she had been in the gym for four hours.

ALEX: I barely last four minutes.

ENZO: And, of course, we told bad blind jokes.

ALEX: A blind man walks into a bar. That's the joke.

ENZO: Henrik was a sensitive soul; Vivian had a wicked sense of humour.

ALEX: Vivian, you crack me up. Ha ha.

ENZO: And we laughed.

ALEX: Ha ha, that happens to me all the time!

ENZO: It was as if we'd known each other for years.

ALEX: It's like we've known each other for years!

ENZO: After dinner we walked Henrik to a taxi and left Vivian with a group of friends at a nearby pub. She disappeared through doors into a wave of oom-pah-pah, oom-pah-pah.

Alex gets up and starts to polka.

ALEX: Vivian and Henrik! I can travel thousands and thousands of miles and find my people. It's like blindness is its own global village, a neighbourhood all over the world.
  It's Octoberfest and I love the music!
  Oom-pah-pah, oom-pah-pah.
  Hey, Enzo, do you know how to polka?

ENZO: Yeah, you taught me this morning.

ALEX: Yes, because you finally showed up to rehearse it! ... Come on over here and dance with me before I slam into something ... Oom-pah-pah, oom-pah-pah ... Oh no!

ENZO: What?

ALEX: I forgot to wear my sports bra ... Oom-pah-pah, oom-pah-pah.
  Let's stop.
  Michael and I went back to our Airbnb.
  Enzo, could you please boo/yeah me to my bed.

He does.

  Yay! It's my bed, I'm going to go to sleep now. And I've had a darn good day.
  Back in my room, I lay on my bed and listened. Being a Friday night, there was more sound outside my window. The mattress, bed frame, pillow, still here. I thought about the day. Collecting information, mapping out place, listening to the choir, and to all the stories that Vivian and Henrik told me ...

I thought about James Holman and his question: 'Does not every traveller rely on others for a good proportion of the information they collect?'

Yes! Yes, James.

Good night, Enzo.

ENZO: Good night, Alex.

Alex lies down on the chest/bed. An alarm dings. Alex sits up.

ALEX: Good morning. Part 3. October 9, 2014. It was Saturday in Freiberg. I stood by a window and listened. Voices. Lots of them filling the street below. I wanted to step out into that sound, that weekend energy, by myself. So, I said to Michael, 'I'm going out on my own.' Enzo?

ENZO: Yes, Alex?

ALEX: Do you know why I wanted to go out by myself?

ENZO: Um. Michael wasn't feeling well?

ALEX: No. Michael was fine.

ENZO: Is it something to do with what you said before? About foolish risks and smart risks?

ALEX: Sort of. I'm going out because I want to.

ENZO: Good reason.

ALEX: And because I seek information and momentum.

ENZO: Just like James.

ALEX: Not safety and protection. So I'll say: Catch ya later. Off I go.

ENZO: Off you go.

ALEX: Off I go. Into Freiberg, which is also the lobby, by myself. And goodbye.

Alex turns.

> Enzo, where's the door?

Enzo gives instructions.

ALEX: Could you just turn my body so I'm straight in line with the door.

Enzo moves Alex.

> Okay, all by myself. Here I go. Going outside.

Alex pulls at the door.

> No, little Alex, you're blind and it's dark and dangerous.
> But, Mommy, I'm fifty-something years old and I want to go outside.
> No, no, no, you can't see a thing, and you'll get lost and fall into a hole.
> But, Mommy, Mommy, if I fall into a hole I'll learn how to climb out and maybe even get a big voice like you.
> No, no, no, Little Blind Alex.

ENZO: Uhh … It's a push …

ALEX: Yes, Enzo, I know it's a push, I am performing.
> I'm trying to say something about fear.
> I want to go outside. And I feel afraid. But I can't tell where the fear is coming from. Did I learn it? Is it mine? Should I get in front of it or kneel down to it? Is it keeping me safe or stuck?

ENZO: Wow. Did James Holman write about that?

ALEX: Mr. Rope-Swinging Big Man? Write about fear? Fear and vulnerability were not his thing.

ENZO: But what about –

ALEX: You know, I'd love to chat about this more, but it's an eighty-minute show and Wheel-Trans is coming. And they don't wait. So I need to get back to me and going outside.

ENZO: Did you end up outside?

ALEX: Yes. Nice segue, Enzo. I decided to get in front of my fear. Freiberg. I stepped outside.

Alex stands still.

Voices engulfed me, from left and right – not a hint of English in the air, random speech sounds drawing closer, then blowing across my face as if in the wind. Once the wind died down, I stuck out my cane and walked.

In the distance, the noise of something thudding caught my attention.

I raced through my mind, trying to find an idea to contain it –

A ladder falling over? Someone hammering something? A small horse? I stepped closer and realized the noise was low to the ground.

It became rhythmic, and people cheered.

Dancing! With wooden shoes. Wooden clogs. Clog dancing!!

The noise became a sound, the sound became an idea, and the idea became a freedom.

People started clapping. I clap too. The universal sound of belonging.

Alex goes to mic, sets mic on stand.

A few hours later, Michael and I took a train to Heidelberg, to meet a tour guide named Suzanne. On meeting Suzanne, she put a walnut in my hand.

'What's in your hand, Alex?' she said.

'Well, Suzanne, it's a walnut.'

'That's amazing,' she said.

'Not really,' I said. 'A walnut usually feels like a walnut.'

Then she took my hand and slapped it on just about everything. Here, Alex, here's a church, *slap*, here's a window, *slap*, here's a door, *slap*, here's a pew, *slap*, here's a book, *slap*, here's a cushion, *slap*, here's a candle, *ouch*, a billy goat, *slap*, Captain Kirk, *slap*, Eight Lords a Leaping, Nine Ladies Dancing, *slap*, *slap*, *slap*, *slap*, *slap* … and an organ –

Perceptual Archaeology (or How to Travel Blind) | 231

A beautiful incredible pipe organ.

Sound of an organ. Alex listens. She sings.

Michael and I stood waiting on the station platform. The handle of my wheelie bag in my right hand and Michael standing to my left. I noted the distinct coming of winter chill in the air. The rising clack of an approaching train as it pulled in toward us. Its brakes squealed, and for a brief moment all went quiet.

Then, chaos.

Voices shouted, something banged, people burst from the train, surging toward us.

The voices advanced and broke into a chant, a drunken chant, louder and closer …

'Michael?'

The voices circled and Michael's arm pulled away.

'Michael?' I lost Michael.

Bodies shoved and pushed. And the bag in my hand – someone kicked my bag.

'Michael? Michael?' Where's Michael?

'I'm over here,' he shouted. 'I'll get us on the train.'

'Michael?'

'Hold on. Stay close,' he said. 'We're nearly at the door.'

I told Michael to get on first.

'But there's a gap,' he said, 'a really big gap.'

'Just go. Just go!'

Michael threw our bags and jumped on board.

First whistle sound.

I reached out.

'Oh God.'

I felt his hand and jumped.

Second whistle sound and door closing.

On board.

A swaying motion. I was inside the train. I felt my feet on the floor, I felt my chest unlock for breath, felt my feet, my breath, felt my feet, felt my breath, my breath.

Enzo?

ENZO: Yes, Alex?

ALEX: What's next?

ENZO: A ferry journey.

ALEX: A ferry journey. A ferry journey up the Rhine and then a taxi, another taxi, and a castle, more stone slapping, a ruin, a hill, a new city, a new Airbnb. I told Michael to go out without me. I didn't wanna go. I didn't wanna go beyond these walls, more new walls.

Where am I? Where in the world am I?

I'm by a kitchen in Cologne.

Could you do this next bit, please?

ENZO: Are you okay?

ALEX: I don't know.

ENZO: Okay … So, Alex writes, I thought about the previous few days – the men at the train station.

ALEX: So loud.

ENZO: Endless slapping of buildings and ruins …

ALEX: Endless.

ENZO: Meaningless lists of words …

ALEX: I'm not having a good time.

ENZO: It occurred to me that I wasn't having a good time.

ALEX: I Just said that.

Alex goes to the bed by herself.

ENZO: When Michael returned, he told me he'd wandered into the city square and there were police in riot gear, broken bottles, people shouting.

Sound begins.

    We checked the news. Football fans and members of the German far right clashed *(sound)* with riot police. *(sound)*

Long silence. Piano music plays.

    The next evening, we set out to enjoy piano music ...
    After the concert, Michael and I walked back to our flat. It was dark, or as Michael described it, deep dark.
    Without warning, the noise of a busy intersection erupted. Sounds of traffic bounced and echoed with the distinct consequence of evening rain.

Alex joins in on this text.

    Noise of engines, smaller, larger, faster, seemed to be coming at me from all directions, and I felt Michael's arm pull back from the intensity.
    He tried to explain how the traffic was working, but I couldn't understand. Headlights flashed in my face, sudden beams appeared on my left, then right, then in front, possibly real, possibly hallucinations. I wanted to run; I couldn't run. I put my hands over my face and gripped Michael's arm. What happened next, I don't remember, but we did make it back to the flat.

ALEX: I went to sleep, a terrible sleep, I had nightmares of planes falling from the sky. I woke up and thought about the plan for the day – an art exhibition, shops, and cafés. Another castle!
    No ... no.
    No way, no, no, no ... No way.

ENZO: Forty-eight hours later I was back at home in London.

ALEX: Forty-eight hours later I was back at home in London.

For three days I did nothing. Nothing. Other than lie under a duvet listening to an audio book by Joan Rivers called *I Hate Everyone ... Starting with Me*. I hate that I didn't make it to Berlin. I hate writing this. I hate having big ideas. I hate castles, I hate ruins, and I hate loud men on train platforms. I hate glorifying dead British men, even if they are blind. I hate feeling vulnerable and fragile instead of bold and strong. I hate how I value bold and strong over vulnerable and fragile. I hate stories about men climbing ships and swinging off ropes because it's inspiring. I hate inspiring. I hate ever thinking I could travel blind.

December 23, 2014. Christmas. *(Alex crawls onto the floor)* Enzo, I need my pillow!

ENZO: Are you going to stay lying on the floor?

ALEX: Yes! I am.

Part Four. Toronto, Canada. Yup. Failure. I ran away from England, back to where it all started. I hid in a Toronto sublet. Fail.

What happened in Germany was more than a travel ambition gone wrong. It felt deeply personal, somehow a comment on who I was or, more acutely, who I was not. I was not James Holman; I was not a navy officer. I was not a man. I was not free to wander the world without vulnerability or fear. Oh my god, it's all coming back to me.

I have spent my entire adult life trying to understand what it means to be blind. Or just how to be blind in a world not designed for me. What happened to everything else? All the rest of me. As a pronoun, as a person, as a fifty-something, single lesbian with no life! Shit!

Oh, Enzo, I'm so sorry.

ENZO: It's okay.

ALEX: No, it's not. You didn't sign up for this.

ENZO: It's okay, really. And that stuff you said about having no life, that's not true.

Alex pats the floor.

ALEX: Can you just … come here … next to me … but don't say anything.

Enzo takes Alex's hand.

>Oh, Enzo, you're holding my hand.

ENZO: I'm here for you, Alex.

ALEX: I know you are. Thank you. Enzo?

ENZO: Yes.

ALEX: What's my next line?

Enzo rushes back to his line-feeding script.

> I was not willing to put the entire failed travel experience behind me and move on. I wanted to dig into it, understand what had happened. So, in fact, I didn't run and hide in a Toronto sublet; I incubated.
>
> December 27, 2014. A snowstorm outside, I opened my computer and wrote this question:
>
> What was I thinking?
>
> How could I have imagined that I could possibly travel through eight cities in less than two weeks, while blind, in a country I'd never been to before?
>
> I listened back to the question using my screen reader.
>
> And realized the answer was in the question.
>
> But the question was not how could I have imagined, but how did I imagine.
>
> I was imagining with my sighted brain – imagining what travelling to new cities and places would look like, imagining places in pictures, with shapes and faces and colours.

It amazed me. I'd moved away from seeing years ago. But my imagination never left home. My imagination was stuck in my sighted past.

I wrote two more words: Blind Imagining.

Imagining what travelling could sound or feel like; decentring vision from my mind.

Alex stands.

A few months later, Michael and I were back on a plane – not to follow James Holman, but to follow my ears and go where my blind imaginings took me. I was off to the music belt of America.

Airplane sound with music of location.

Within minutes of our arrival in Atlanta, I had been called 'sunshine,' 'baby,' 'sweet pea,' 'ma'am.'

We set off on an easy afternoon stroll and came across a church – not just any church, the church led by Martin Luther King Sr. and Jr. in the 1950s.

The sound of gospel singing, like human thunder, guided my ears and soul to the sanctuary. I stood where they stood and sang where they sang.

Gospel music plays. Alex sings along to the gospel music.

We crossed the street and climbed the stairs, which is also the ladder, to visit the Martin Luther King Freedom Garden. Beautiful birdsong. Roses, hundreds of roses, filling the air. And freshly cut grass. And a circle of plaques, freedom plaques, written by children from all over the world. Michael read them to me.

Mohammed Sied

Freedom

A dream I want to come true.

Rohan Iqbal

Where I live, we need peace, peace that gives us faith and courage.

Sasha Ward

Something to reach for – still high in the sky.
Freedom.
Later Michael and I hit the highway in a rental car for our road trip to Nashville, Tennessee.

Alex car improv, get in car, shut the door, etc.

You know why I love road trips so much, Enzo?

ENZO: No, but I hope you'll tell me.

ALEX: I love listening to the radio. All the banter, the songs – it tells me so much about a place.

Alex mimes changing stations. Short bits of songs play – they all are about Jesus.

I turned the dial again and again until finally, thank Jesus, Whitney saved me.

'I Want to Dance with Somebody' plays. Alex mimes driving.

Driving and driving, and driving, driving, driving. Hit the gas, hit the clutch, driving, driving, driving. And dancing and driving and … I can dance and drive at the same time, it's my extrasensory power!

Alex stands and dances … Sound of a siren.

Shit, it's the cops!

She sits and mimes taking the wheel and gearing down.

That was close. Good thing they didn't catch me driving without my white cane.

Alex hits the brakes.

What a great road trip.

Leaves the car and slams the door.

Finally, Nashville, Tennessee!

I stepped into a world of sound, a mountain of sound. It dominated my ears the way the Rocky Mountains dominate the eye … Music, everywhere.

Music grows.

Michael and I walked along the main street, passing different clubs, one after the other. Broadway Brewhouse, Bootleggers Inn, Whiskey Bent Saloon, Tequila Cowboy, Layla's Hillbilly Store, and settled in with a more mellow act at Jimmy's Feed and Seed.

Alex sways in circles.

That night I walked back to the Airbnb; no, I sang my way back.

Alex slow-dances by herself.

Hey, Enzo, you wanna slow-dance?

ENZO: Umm, err, I don't think …

ALEX: No, no, I mean over there, by yourself.

ENZO: Oh, right.

ALEX: At your station …

ENZO: Right, right.

ALEX: That's funny, you thought … with me … No, no. Phew.

ENZO: Close one.

Enzo slow-dances.

ALEX: Yeah. Later, I lay in my bed and felt like the world was as if I had designed it. As if I had designed it.

ENZO: That's cool.

ALEX: I think so too. Thanks, Enzo.

ENZO: You're welcome.

ALEX: Enough slow-dancing. Could I have a round of applause, please?

Audience applause.

>Thank you.
>Enzo, could you boo/yeah me ... Now, hey, let's get the audience to do it.

She reminds the audience how it works and warms them up. Then goes using audience 'boos' and 'yeahs' to find the chair.

>Enzo, it's banjolele time. Could you bring my banjolele?

ENZO: *(bursting into a Southern accent)* I sure can. Here I come.

ALEX: Enzo, what's happened to you?

ENZO: My name is Dwayne. I'm your roadie. Every musician in Tennessee has a roadie.

ALEX: I'm scared.

ENZO: Don't be scared. Every musician in Nashville's gotta have a roadie with a voice like this.

ALEX: Okay, Dwayne. That evening Michael and I met with five members of an adult social group for blind people. We met at Gayle and Peggy's house.

ENZO: Gayle and Peggy. Them's two ladies who can't see too well. They're so nice.

ALEX: They're blind like me.

ENZO: You're blind? That means you can't see how pretty I am.

ALEX: I'll learn to cope ...

ALEX: We met at Peggy's house. We talked about our lives – the things that are hard and the things that bring joy – time with friends, dancing, tandem cycling, singing and travel.

Peggy had, in fact, been a travel agent before she lost her sight. Gayle had just travelled across Europe with a blind friend.

She said that her sighted neighbour, Bill, asked what she could possibly get out of travelling. 'Bill,' she said, 'I am not dead.'

Alex sings 'Don't Fence Me In,' and Enzo joins in for the last verse.

ALEX: Part Five. June 2015, Graceland.

The music belt of America was becoming a healing belt for me. Six days had passed since I'd arrived, slow-paced days, time and place not only made sense but supported sense – I took the time I needed to listen and hear, my mind wasn't racing to keep up with the immediacy of sight or lost in a perceptual nowhere.

A logic of location existed directly and almost entirely through my ears, with sound and music.

Michael wanted to do a tour of Graceland, the home of the King. I considered the joy of hearing, 'Now that chair over there is where Elvis ate banana sandwiches and that chair is where Priscilla sneezed.'

I decided I'd give the tour a pass, hang out in the Airbnb, feel around for some kind of stereo system, and listen to my favourite Elvis tracks. Hey, what's this?

Alex listens and sings along to 'Suspicious Minds' using a voice modulator.

After singing with Elvis, I checked my emails. There was a message from the funders, the original funders of all this travel. The message read: 'Dear Alex, thank you for your recent update on your travel writing project. As we the British blah blah blah funded you to travel in the footsteps of one of our national heroes, James Holman, we'd like to know why you are in a rental car driving across America.' I wondered how I'd solve this one. And when we wonder we google. I googled: James Holman America travel writing. And the name of an American historian came up. Yes. A university guy who had studied James Holman and knew lots about lots. I found an article about Holman's antics up the masts of ships – remember, all that rope-swinging hoohah?

The article described that every sailing expedition for James Holman started with a stunt. He'd throw off his coat, toss his cane aside, and swing out over the sea. One mistake and he'd plunge to his death. The historian guy claimed that James did this as a performance, not as an act of bravado but as an act of control – an attempt to, quote, cure his fellow shipmates from seeing him as an invalid, end quote.

Now, that sounds like vulnerability to me.

I started to consider James Holman with a touch more grace.

Grace-land. Thank you, Elvis.

And hello again, James.

Is it true? Were you performing yourself? Performing heroics for validity? Were you more afraid of your shipmates' attitudes than drowning at sea? If so, I get it. I wish I didn't, but I do.

Or, forget the historian, maybe you just loved swinging around, climbing stuff, being up high. Up high – the sky has no walls.

I wish you could time-travel, James, and be here tonight. I'd say: Ditch the uniform, put on some jeans, join me and the audience in the bar, and let's swap travel stories.

Enzo, did I ever tell you I used to drive a motorcycle?

ENZO: I think you mentioned it in Part One.

ALEX: I love it. I still have it. It's in my mother's barn.

ENZO: I'm glad you still have it.

ALEX: Thanks, so am I. One day, I'll have my motorcycle in my living room and hang plants off it.

ENZO: Wow, I'd love to see that.

ALEX: Maybe you will! Maybe you'll come over. We'll have tea and water the plants. Together.

ENZO: Nice. I'm smiling.

ALEX: I'm smiling.

ENZO: So, how did you respond to the funders?

ALEX: I said a historian expert claimed James Holman travelled to every inhabited continent in the world. Badda bing!

ENZO: Bada boom!

ALEX: Going to the southern states, engaging with my ears, I found a sense of hope. I tried imagining again, blind imagining, what travelling might sound or feel like. What travelling might feel like. I imagined my feet on the ground. Across grass, across earth, across flat and uneven. I imagined space and geography through balance and bone.

James Holman, my new friend in jeans, understood this. And he needed only six words to express it: 'I see better with my feet.'

On September 10, 2015, I was on a plane to Portugal, the starting point of a very long walk to Santiago de Compostela, one of many ancient routes known as the Camino Trail.

Our plane landed in Porto. Michael and I went straight to a patio, a café called Lembrar, Portuguese for 'remember.' Enzo, please would you guide me to a seat on patio Lembrar, which is also the front row? How lucky that there is an empty seat. Was it something I said? Here we are in Porto. Did anyone come here to try its famous fortified wine? Enzo, I think it's time to enjoy a little glass of port.

ENZO: I was thinking exactly the same. Here, please allow me to pour – so you enjoy.

ALEX: Very nice.

Alex talks to the people next to her.

Enzo, perhaps see if my friends in the café would like a little glass of port.

Enzo offers port.

ENZO: You know, the special thing about this café is that everyone who enters gets a little something to hold, a little stone, to help you remember.

ALEX: That's good because after this drink I won't remember a thing.

ENZO: Did everyone get something to hold when you came into the theatre, which is now a café? Let's all hold it now. Is there anyone else who'd like a glass of port?

ALEX: Lucky you, you get to hold a glass of port while everyone else holds a rock.

ENZO: Would anyone else like a little glass of port?

ALEX: Enzo, budget, budget. Arts council. I think we should move on to our next day …

ENZO: Already?

ALEX: Day two, a very early morning rise.
 And the start of our Camino journey, a 120-kilometre walk across Portugal and Spain.
 We laced up our boots, got our Camino passport stamped, and off we go.
 First kilometre.

Sound of rain.

 Rain.

Rain pours.

 Pouring rain. The rain bounced off cobblestones, windows, and buildings in the town square, actually bringing shape and place to this small Portuguese village.

Rain continues – Alex remains sitting in the audience, listening.

At the edge of the village, I held on to Michael's backpack and stepped directly behind him. The Camino pathways had washed away, leaving only currents of water.

At one point, Michael told me to keep my feet in very tightly, because we were walking across the top of a very narrow wall.

Footsteps, distant waterfall, occasional voice.

Twenty-eighth kilometre. We walked. The day brought sunshine and fellow walkers from all over the globe – a couple from Australia, a photographer from Belgium, an anaesthetist from Phoenix, a blind woman and her girlfriend from Amsterdam. Yay … I'm not the only blind gay in the Camino village.

Sounds continue – Alex listens.

Fifty-seventh kilometre. We walked. There were, along the way, little roadside tavernas, often in the middle of nowhere, offering relief for basic liquid in and liquid out. Occasionally, these unexpected spaces turned remarkable, with the swing of a door. The doors would open and the voice of a fellow walker, someone we'd not walked with for three or four days, suddenly appeared with a heartfelt 'Michael and Alex!' The middle of nowhere became the middle of everywhere.

Alex listens.

Seventy-ninth kilometre. Walking.
This long sense of movement and quiet thought.
Only my breath and body through space. The angle of my body as we turned – Michael's arm, my bones and breath while we turned.
We turn.
Then people. A community.
A parade into a small church. Bagpipes.
A bell. Singing.
Then quiet. Just the up and down of the land.

A little bug up my neck.
A long piece of grass.
A hole in my sock.
Walking.
A man calls out, 'Bon camino!' 'Hello, bon camino.'
'Well, thanks, you're amazing too.'
Some birds, some little houses,
A waterfall.
Way over there, another church bell. And my hips might be hurting.

ENZO: Alex?

ALEX: Yes, Michael?

ENZO: Would you like a break?

ALEX: Yes. Thank you. Let's sit down somewhere on the roadside.

ENZO: Good idea. Here's my arm. Here's a good spot to sit.

ALEX: Michael and I sat on the side of the road, next to a little cemetery.
And he hands me a little stone.
'This is what the roofs are made of,' he says.
The stone feels dusty.
'It's kind of red,' he says, 'kind of coral.'
And he gives me another stone.
'It's kind of red,' I say, 'kind of coral.'
And we walk.
And I don't pay attention like I'm used to paying attention. Nothing is 'paid' here.
It's received. Absorbed.
This might sound epic, but it's not. It's simple.
Walking.
One-hundred-and-fifth kilometre. We walked. By the final day I was limping. My hips hurt, my toes were blistered, and I walked with a

stick I'd found in the woods. Despite the pain, I didn't want the journey to end.

Through the final hour, through a thick wood on the edge of Santiago, I noticed everything, felt each footstep against the ground, each tree, root, and rock, heard every scuttle of leaves, snap of twigs. I wanted to remember every sound I could hear. Like a photograph in my ears.

James Holman found his own words for such moments. He wrote:

'In the deep of the green wood, in the wind of the hills, there was an intelligence. It entered my heart and I could have wept, not that I did not see, but that I could not portray all that I felt.'

Fifteen years of friendship with Michael, twenty-four hours after walking into Santiago, sixteen weeks since hitting the road in Tennessee, eleven months after stepping out of a taxi into Freiburg, and eighteen years since Winkie inspired me into an L.A. pool, I sat quietly next to my friend Michael – no, *with* my friend Michael – in A Coruña Airport.

ENZO: Do you feel proud of yourself??

ALEX: Yes, I do.
And then there was silence.

A moment of silence.

    Silence. Nowhere and everywhere.
    Thank you for listening to my talk. The end.

Music – 'Don't Fence Me In.'

The Editors

Alex Bulmer has been progressing Disabled-led creativity since the early 1990s, when she worked with the UK's Graeae Theatre, CBC Television's Disability Network, cofounded Dis-This Collective, and the Picasso Project. She finished the twentieth century with her play *Smudge*, acclaimed for its crip and queer aesthetics. A BAFTA, Dora, and Sony Award–nominated writer, she cofounded Cripping the Stage and the CoMotion Festival, and leads Unsightly Arts (formerly Fire and Rescue), whose work decentres sight from imagination to creation.

Debbie Patterson is a Winnipeg-based actor, playwright, director, dramaturge, and mother. She is a proud advocate for Disability justice through her work as founding and current Artistic Director of Sick + Twisted Theatre. She is passionate about supporting the development of Disabled theatre-makers, the creation of new works by Disabled artists, and bringing the lived experience of Disability into mainstream theatre spaces. She is a recipient of the King Charles III's Coronation Medal, the United Nations Platform for Action Committee's Activist of the Year Award, and the City of Winnipeg's Making a Mark Award.

The Contributors

Patty Berne was the co-founder, executive director, and artistic director of Sins Invalid and a Fellow of the Ford Foundation's Disability Futures Forum. Their work spanned advocacy for immigrants and asylum seekers, community organizing with the Haitian diaspora, supporting survivors of state and interpersonal violence through trauma-focused clinical psychology, working alongside young people in the prison system to imagine alternatives to criminal legal systems, and championing Disability and LGBTQI perspectives in reproductive genetic technologies. They are widely recognized for their work in establishing the framework and practice of Disability Justice.

Dawn Jani Birley, recipient of the King Charles III Coronation Medal 2025, is an award-winning Deaf actor, movement artist, translator, and theatre consultant. Born in Saskatchewan to a third-generation Deaf family, she proudly identifies as culturally and linguistically Deaf. Renowned for her powerful portrayal of Horatio in *Prince Hamlet*, Birley founded 1S1 Theatre to bring more Deaf-led narratives and multifaceted performances to the stage. She currently serves as a theatre professor at the newly established Deaf Arts Academy (DAA), created by the Canadian Cultural Society of the Deaf to expand opportunities for Deaf artists across Canada.

Yolanda Bonnell *(They/She)* is a Queer, Two-Spirit Anishinaabe-Ojibwe, South Asian mixed-race storyteller. Hailing from Fort William First Nation, Ontario, their arts practice is now based in Tkarón:to. In 2020, Yolanda's four-time-Dora-nominated solo piece *bug* was remounted at Theatre Passe Muraille while the published play was shortlisted for a Governor General's Literary Award. She has also won the Playwright's Guild of Canada Tom Hendry Drama Award for the play *My Sister's Rage*. Yolanda, who has just completed her first full-length young adult novel, proudly bases her arts practice in Anishinaabe methodologies, working toward Disability Justice in theatre.

Audrey-Anne Bouchard is a stage director and lighting designer. She completed a BFA in Theatre Design at Concordia University and a master's degree in Theory and Practice of Dance and Theatre at Université de Nice. Inspired by her situation as a person living with low vision, she initiated the research project Au-delà du visuel in 2016 to create immersive performances that involve all of the audience's senses but sight, and are therefore accessible to people who are blind, partially sighted, and sighted. She and her team developed and presented the shows *Camille* (2019) and *Fragments: celle qui m'habitait déjà* (2025). For *Camille*, Audrey-Anne received the META award for Outstanding Direction and the Monique Lefebvre Universal Accessibility Award. Audrey-Anne also works as an accessibility consultant for artists and organizations and as a teacher at the National Theatre School of Canada. https://audeladuvisuel.com

Vivi Dabee is a lover of the arts. Her enthusiasm for literature and theatre led her to the world of academia where she studied theatre and completed her English BA (Honours) at the University of Winnipeg and her Master's of English at the University of Manitoba. Vivi is a poet, playwright, and vocalist. She is passionate about telling stories that interrogate race and racial identity and creating art that both represents and explores the lived experience of blindness. She is co-host of the podcasts *The Lens: Living Diverse* and *The Blind Truth* and is the audio-description consultant for Vocal Image Ensemble Winnipeg (VIEW). Her credits include *Passing*, *Vivi's Vision*, *Antigone*, and *Neither Here nor There*.

Raven Davis is a multidisciplinary artist, curator, educator, and human rights speaker born and raised in Toronto, Ontario. A creative practitioner in contemporary art and performance, Davis investigates land-based, archival, and spiritual practices with calls to action, transformative justice,

The Contributors | 251

social change, and healing. Their works include movement, visual art, sound, video, and performance. Davis incorporates critical discourse, historical inquiries, addressing race, colonization, slavery, the environment, disability, spirituality, and Two-Spirit and transgender identities within their practice.

JD Derbyshire was a leading figure in Disability and Mad Arts whose vision and mentorship have left a lasting impact on Canada's artistic landscape. Over their decades-long career, JD worked across theatre, literature, film, comedy, and visual art, continually challenging conventions and redefining integrated artistic practice. They are known for their award-winning one-person show *Certified* and their novel *Mercy Gene: the Man-Made Making of a Mad Woman*. Their generosity, humour, and belief in learning and creating beyond traditional systems inspired many. A bold advocate for equity, diversity, inclusion, and access, JD helped shape spaces where artists could thrive on their own terms.

Chris Dodd is a Treaty 6–based (Edmonton) award-winning Deaf actor, playwright, accessibility advocate, and Governor General's Innovation Award finalist. He is the founder and artistic director of SOUND OFF, Canada's national festival devoted to Deaf performance, which has been running annually since 2017. Chris holds a degree from the University of Alberta's Drama program and has been working within Edmonton's theatre community, and across Canada, for over twenty-five years. His play *Deafy* has been touring across Canada and internationally since 2021. It has been published by Playwrights Canada Press as part of the anthology *Interdependent Magic: Disability Performance in Canada*, making him the first Deaf playwright to be published by that organization.

Other notable theatre performances include the role of Alphonse in *Ultrasound* at Theatre Passe Muraille. Film credits include the role of Odin in the feature film *Finality of Dusk*. In 2019, he was the recipient of the Guy Laliberté Prize for innovation and creative leadership by the Canada Council for the Arts.

Born in Jakarta, Indonesia and living in Toronto, Canada, **Karina Iskandarsjah** is an artist and curator who creates work about grief, memory, borders, cultural hybridity, activism, and ecology. She has an MFA in Criticism and Cultural Studies from OCAD University; was an associate curator at Trinity Square Video; and has worked with many spaces including Vtape, Inter/Access, Critical Distance, and Xpace Cultural Centre. Currently, she is a research project manager at Surface Impression, a member of Artists Against Artwashing, and co-host of 'Make Good,' a year-long production residency for artists and food professionals.

Niall McNeil is a multidisciplinary artist who identifies with Down Syndrome. He has been involved with theatre from an early age. Niall recently wrote and directed a new play, *Beauty and the Beast: My Life*, in 2025, which won a Jessie Richardson Theatre Award for Significant Achievement: Artistic Innovation in Theatrical Form. Niall directed his first documentary film *The Originals*, which premiered at the 2024 DOXA Film Festival. Niall lives in Vancouver, BC.

Maria R. Palacios, known artistically as the 'Goddess on Wheels,' is a Houston-based poet, author, and disability justice activist. A veteran of the 1990 'Capitol Crawl,' her work explores the intersections of disability, gender, sexuality, and her identity as a Latina immigrant. Since 2007, she has performed with Sins Invalid and authored several books, including *Criptionary*. Palacios remains a leading voice in advocacy, focusing on empowerment for women with disabilities and crip survival.

Born in Vancouver in 1986, **Salima Punjani** is a self-taught multisensory artist who uses mediums like soft sculpture, vibrotactile, spatial sound, field recordings, digital video and photography, and relational aesthetics. Her artistic approach is intertwined with her interest in trauma-informed care and disability justice. A common thread through all of her work is the creation of environments that allow for receptivity of connection. She is particularly interested in how multiple senses can be used to expand the possibilities for people to feel welcome in art spaces as well as to create artful experiences of empathy, intimacy, and connection. Her recent work explores themes such as pleasure, grief, rest as resistance to systemic injustice, and how medical data can be subverted into finding human connection rather than pathologies.

She holds a BA in Communications and Political Science from Carleton University, a Graduate Diploma in Journalism from Concordia University, and a Master's in Social Work from McGill University with research focusing on the intersection of the arts and care work.

Theodore Walker Robinson (Hon. BA, MA, MA) is a Black, Low Vision, Hard-of-Hearing weaver, singer, musician, researcher and nonprofit executive working in arts administration. Based in Toronto, Ontario, they are the co-founder of the Disability Collective, a nonprofit consulting agency championing accessibility in art, culture, and performance. Their research practice involves exploring blind and low vision pedagogies as they relate to creative skills training and education for the visually impaired. Theodore is an Access Advisor for the City of Mississauga, the City of Toronto, and the Luminato Festival Toronto. Theodore's passion lies in mentorship for Black, transgender, and Disabled emerging artists and leaders in Canadian art and culture.

Alice Sheppard is a movement artist and writer. Alice creates movement that emerges from her understanding of disabled expression, seeking to find the maximum expression of disability in all her different embodiments. Engaging with Disability Arts, culture, and history, Alice's commissioned work attends to the complex intersections of disability, gender, and race. Her dance and disability writing has appeared in the *New York Times*, peer-reviewed essay collections, and academic journals. Alice is the founder and Artistic Director of Kinetic Light, a Disability Arts organization based in New York City. Kinetic Light makes transformative art that affirms the intersectional Disability Arts movement.

Dr. Syrus Marcus Ware is a Vanier Scholar, visual artist, activist, curator, and educator. Syrus is an Assistant Professor at the School of the Arts, McMaster University. Using drawing, installation, theatre/performance, Syrus works with social justice frameworks and Black activist culture. His work was part of the inaugural Toronto Biennial of Art in both 2019 and 2022 [*Antarctica* and *Ancestors, Do You Read Us? (Dispatches from the Future* and MBL:*Freedom*)]. Syrus holds a doctorate from York University in the Faculty of Environmental Studies. He is the co-editor of the best-selling *Until We Are Free: Reflections on Black Lives Matter in Canada* (URP, 2020). Syrus is a co-founder of Black Lives Matter–Canada and the Wildseed Centre for Art & Activism.

Typeset in Albertina and Barlow.

Printed at the Coach House on bpNichol Lane in Toronto, Ontario, on fsc-certified Sustana recycled paper, which was manufactured in Saint-Jérôme, Quebec. This book was printed with vegetable-based ink on a 1973 Heidelberg KORD offset litho press. Its pages were folded on a Baumfolder, gathered by hand, bound on a Sulby Auto-Minabinda, and trimmed on a Polar single-knife cutter.

Coach House Books is situated on occupied land, which is the traditional territory of several Indigenous nations, including the Mississaugas of the Credit (an Anishnabek people), the Haudenosaunee Confederacy, and the Wendat and Petun nations, and is now home to many First Nations, Inuit, and Métis people. This land is covered by the Dish With One Spoon Covenant, an agreement between different First Nations communities to share resources peacefully and equitably, and by the Two-Row Wampum, a covenant of mutual respect and non-interference between early settlers and the Haudenosaunee. The land is also subject to Treaty 13, sometimes called the Toronto Purchase, signed between the settler colonists and the Mississaugas of the Credit.

As a settler organization, we acknowledge that we have violated these treaties and agreements. We acknowledge the grievous and ongoing harm of colonialism, and we strive to work toward a future of justice and reconciliation.

Edited by Alex Bulmer and Debbie Patterson
Cover and interior design by Crystal Sikma

Coach House Books
80 bpNichol Lane
Toronto ON M5S 3J4
Canada

mail@chbooks.com
www.chbooks.com